WALKING OVER THE WAVES

QUINT... ... ... E PIERS

Chris Foote Wood

Whittles Publishing

Published
Whittles Publ
Dunbeath,
Caithness KW6 6EY,
Scotland, UK
www.whittlespublishing.com

© 2008 Chris Foote Wood

ISBN 978-1904445-67-8

Front Cover: Eastbourne Pier (author's collection)
Frontispiece: Children and dog having a paddle at New Brighton
(Frances Foote collection)

Every effort has been made to trace copyright holders and to obtain their permission for
the use of copyright material. The publisher would be grateful if notified of any amendments that should
be incorporated in future reprints or editions of this book.

Printed by Bell & Bain Ltd., Glasgow

CONTENTS

Preface v

Aberystwyth Royal 1

Bangor Garth 4

Beaumaris 6

Blackpool Central 8

Blackpool North 12

Blackpool South 18

Bognor Regis 20

Boscombe 22

Bournemouth 25

Brighton Palace 28

Brighton West 35

Burnham-on-Sea 39

Clacton 41

Cleethorpes 44

Clevedon 47

Colwyn Bay Victoria 50

Cromer 53

Deal 56

Eastbourne 59

Falmouth Prince of Wales 62

Felixstowe 64

Fleetwood Victoria 66

Gravesend Town 69

Great Yarmouth Britannia 71

Great Yarmouth Wellington 73

Hastings 76

Herne Bay 78

Hythe 81

Llandudno 85

Lowestoft Claremont 88

Lowestoft South 90

Mumbles 93

Paignton 95

Penarth 97

Ramsey Queens 102

Ryde 105

St Annes 109

Saltburn 112

Sandown Culver 117

Skegness 123

Southend-on-Sea 126

Southport 133

Southsea Clarence 138

Southsea South Parade 140

Southwold 142

Swanage 146

Teignmouth Grand 149

Torquay Princess 151

Totland Bay 153

Walton-on-the-Naze 156

Weston-super-Mare Birnbeck 158

Weston-super-Mare Grand 162

Weymouth Commercial/Pleasure 165

Weymouth Pier Bandstand 169

Worthing 171

Yarmouth 176

Acknowledgements 180

About the Author 181

National Piers Society 182

List of Piers by Region 183

Other books by Chris Foote Wood 184

References and further reading 185

PREFACE

Piers have fascinated me from the moment I first trod the deck of Blackpool's North Pier as a very small boy with my nana and grandad. The imposing entrance, the exotic buildings, the unusual structure, the crowds, the razzmatazz, the shops, the cafés, the ice cream parlours, hucksters and fortune-tellers – and, above all (or rather below): the sea. You could see the sea beneath your feet, and yet feel perfectly safe, indeed brave. You could walk over the waves without a care in the world. I was hooked, and have remained so ever since.

But it wasn't until the year 2007 that I finally set out on my first real "pier crawl" – visiting every seaside pleasure pier in England, Wales and the Isle of Man. There ought to be a name for pier enthusiasts. "Pier spotters" is not quite right, because piers don't move, well, not very much anyway. "Pier crawlers" might not appeal to some, but I like it. Piers are fun, and this is a fun name. Closely related to pier enthusiasts are the hardy breed of "ship spotters", maritime enthusiasts who often make a beeline for piers, especially piers that are situated around the Solent and the Thames Estuary. Armed with their cameras, spotters' guides and binoculars, they study every passing ship with enthusiasm.

Back in 1947, when I asked my nana if we could go on Blackpool's two other piers, and she said, 'no, they're not the sort of places we want to go', I was enthralled. This was my first lesson in the British class system. And so, a social dimension was added to my already heightened curiosity; not just about piers, but about the world in which I found myself. When I learned that other seaside resorts also had piers, I thought: what a wonderful thing it would be to travel all around the coast of Britain and go on every pier in the country.

On a pier, there's always something to do, and usually something to please everybody. Whether it's to enjoy the amusements or appreciate the architecture, every taste is catered for. For a small toll – or more usually for free – you enter another world, a world half-way between the land and the sea yet tied to both. You can patronise the amusements, stroll the deck, take in the views, breathe in the ozone, sunbathe, read, contemplate, go fishing, take a sea trip, have some refreshments, or do any combination of these pleasurable activities. To my mind, there are few things in life as enjoyable as taking your ease with food and drink (alcoholic or otherwise) on a seaside pier.

Chris and Frances Foote Wood, enjoying the sunshine on Brighton Palace Pier

Piers were built to make money. Victorian entrepreneurs saw the possibilities of cashing in from holidaymakers and day-trippers brought to their seaside resorts by the burgeoning railways. The first piers were built primarily as landing stages for sea trips by "steam packet" which were all the rage at the time. It is no coincidence that many pier owners and shareholders also had a stake in railways and ferryboats. But as well as making profit from trains and boats, it quickly became clear that money was to be made from the piers themselves and also from the adjoining shore.

As soon as the first piers were built, people started walking on them for health and recreation, a simple pleasure that endures to this day. The pier owners brought in bands and concert parties to entertain both sea-trippers and pier strollers, and people even began to dance on piers. Piers became fun! At the same time, piers were presented to the public as exotic, magical places. Piers were given an architecture all of their own, with India, China and ancient Egypt as their inspiration. The idea was to create a world out of the ordinary, an exciting world where day-trippers and holidaymakers could forget their day-to-day worries and be transported into a world of enjoyment and wonder.

So there you have it: piers as "another world", piers as profit. Why it has taken me sixty years to realise my dream of visiting every British seaside pier, I cannot explain. But I do know why I've done it now. After making a career change from thirty years working as a freelance journalist running my own press agency to become a full-time author, I wrote a book called *When I'm Sixty-Four*. In it I advise sixty-somethings to *do it now*! So I thought, I had better take my own advice.

In 2007 I set off on my odyssey round the coast of Britain, stopping off at every one of our 56 seaside piers (and quite a few others) on the way. Researching and writing this book has been a thoroughly fascinating, stimulating and memorable experience. I hope it will inspire you to visit more of our wonderful seaside piers … and more often.

Chris Foote Wood
Bishop Auckland

ABERYSTWYTH ROYAL

Aberystwyth Royal Pier, c.1905 (courtesy of the National Piers Society)

FIRST PURPOSE-BUILT PLEASURE PIER IN WALES

This Eugenius Birch pier was the first of its kind in the principality, allowing Aberystwyth, looking out over Cardigan Bay, to call itself 'the Brighton of Wales'. Costing £13,600 the pier opened on Good Friday 1865, the same day that the Cambrian Railway started running trains to the town. More that 7,000 people went on the pier that day.

Unlike most of Britain's seaside piers, Aberystwyth's is built on solid rock foundations. A convenient outcrop allowed Birch to design well holes for the supporting piles which were concreted in.

But disaster struck in January 1866, just a few short months later. The pier was hit by a severe storm which destroyed the end 100 feet of its structure. It took six years for repairs to be completed. Crippled by repair costs and the lack of revenue, the pier company was forced to sell up. In 1872 the new owners built a new pier head with a pavilion and refreshment room. Electric lighting was introduced in 1895. There was enough business to justify adding a 3,000-seat, glass-domed, Gothic-style pavilion at the shore end in 1896 at a cost of £8,000. The Princess of Wales, later to become Queen Alexandra, did the honours on 26 June 1896 with the Prince of Wales, later Edward VII, to earn the pier its 'Royal' title.

There is a connection with the RMS *Titanic* – the 'ship of dreams'. Wallace Henry Hartley (born 1878) from Colne in Lancashire, played his violin on British shores for the last time on Aberystwyth Pier in 1911 before perishing in the 1912 disaster when he famously kept his small orchestra playing until the final moment. That same year, in 1912, the pavilion was converted to a cinema. In 1915 the Borough Council took over the pier on a lease.

There was further storm damage in 1938, reducing the pier to 350 feet, and in 1960 there was a fire on the pier. When the pier was taken over by its present owners Don Leisure Ltd. in 1979,

1

the neck had deteriorated so much so that, other than the pavilion, the pier had to be closed. After repairs and improvements costing half a million pounds, the pier was re-opened in 1968. In 1987 a new restaurant and snooker hall were added.

Plans for a new pier alongside the existing one were approved in 1986, however, it was never built.

Whilst the front end of the pier is thriving, the short remaining neck is sadly closed to the public. The old wooden decking has been covered with metal plates, and half the area is taken up with sheds used for storage and making ice cream. The extensive pavilion, which still shows its fine features above first floor level, houses an amusement arcade, a social and snooker club, and a first-floor restaurant. The Inn on the Pier advertises itself as 'Ceredigion's first and only 24-hour pub'. You can even buy and sell euros on the pier!

There are some interesting old photographs in the side corridors: the pier as it was; a flying-boat in the bay; and the visit of HMS *Repulse* and *Renown* in 1930. There are none of the usual amusements on the promenade, but directly opposite the pier is Pier Street with cafés and shops, including a model shop. There is also ample free parking on the prom.

At the other end of the promenade is another gem – the longest electrical cliff railway in Great Britain at 789 feet long. The journey up and down Constitution Hill takes 4 minutes and 12 seconds, and (it is claimed) never varies by more than a second either way. The railway is unusual in that it has three different gradients; one in four at top and bottom and one in three in the middle. The two cars are connected by a continuous cable looped around a pulley. Originally water-balanced, it was converted to electrical operation in 1921. The cars run on standard four feet, eight and a half-inch British Rail gauge line, hence the need for the operator to blow a whistle at the start of each journey.

Cliff railway – one of the best (author's collection)

The 'toast rack' cars still have their original 1896 chassis, a tribute to Victorian engineering. The railway was designed by George Croydon Marks, who also designed cliff railways at Lynton & Lynmouth, Bridgenorth and Bristol. To construct the Aberystwyth cliff railway, which is all in cutting, 1,200 tons of rock had to be removed and four footbridges built over it to maintain the public footpaths across Constitution Hill. The railway cost £60,000, a huge sum for the time. Opened on Saturday, 1 August 1896, 520 people each paid 8*d.* (the equivalent of £4 today) to travel on it. As the *Aberystwyth Observer* said: "nine out of ten people would rather walk up and down the hill than pay that sum.'

In 1948 the Aberystwyth Pier Company bought the railway, which eventually closed in 1976. Under new ownership, it re-opened on 31 July 1976, only six weeks later. A new camera obscura, replacing the old one, which closed in the1920s, was opened in 1985 and is one good reason to use the railway. On a clear day, it is possible to see 26 mountain peaks, including Mount Snowdon, from the top of the hill. The present owners, Constitution Hill Ltd., are a community-based business and took over in 1998.

Pier pavilion has a plain exterior (author's collection)

CHRIS'S VERDICT: fun at the front, but only half a pier
WALK TIME: n/a

Work started: 1864
First opened: 1865
Designer: Eugenius Birch
Contractor: J E Dowson
Construction: raked cast iron piles concreted into well holes; cast iron trestles under a wooden deck
Original length: 700 ft (214 m)
Present length: 300 ft (91 m)
Storm damage: 1866, 1938
Fire: 1960
Restoration: 1866–72, 1896, 1965/8, 1986/7
Original owners: Aberystwyth Pier Promenade Co.
Present owners: Don Leisure Ltd.
Website: www.royalpier.co.uk

BANGOR GARTH

Bangor Garth Pier – stretching out across the Menai Strait (author's collection)

DELICATE AND DELIGHTFUL

Here is a pier, one of Britain's finest, that has survived a ship collision, closure, planned demolition, and which was sold for a penny! Of delicate and delightful construction, this beautiful pier has been lovingly restored. The wrought iron entrance gates are magnificent, and the whole pier is a gem. My only criticism – apart from the horrible litter bins – is that the pier is *dry*, that is, no alcoholic beverages are allowed. But this is Wales after all. The pier offers stunning scenery all round, with an added bonus when you get to the far end: a view of Thomas Telford's iconic Menai Suspension Bridge.

Stretching two-thirds of the way across the Menai Strait, the pier is enhanced by having both sea and land as a backdrop. The pier has a fine set of ornamental lamps and handrails. There are pairs of elegant, domed kiosks on circular platforms along the pier, and a larger circular pavilion at the pier head which houses a café and toilets. When using the latter facilities, one can view the wind-whipped waves through the planking – very soothing!

Rated as one of the three best seaside piers in the country, Bangor's Grade II* listed pier was opened by Lord Penrhyn on 14 May 1896. It was built to a design by London-based architect, John James Webster, at a cost of £14,475. Apart from a pierrot show, at first there were none of the usual 'amusements' on the pier, although later a kiosk was added. There was a pontoon landing stage serving steamers to and from Blackpool, Douglas (Isle of Man) and Liverpool. Passengers' baggage was hauled along the length of the 1,550 feet (473 metres) pier by a 36-inch gauge rail line.

5,263 people went on the pier on that first day, many coming by train on cheap excursions. There was a procession, of course, headed by the Navy. There followed the Bangor Fire Brigade, the Bangor Artillery Volunteers, the Oddfellows, the Foresters, tradesmen, Bangor Football Club, the mayor and other dignitaries.

In 1914 the cargo steamer SS *Christiana* broke free of her moorings and collided with the pier, doing considerable damage. The Royal Engineers put up a temporary bridge to close the gap, but that was the last of the rail line and the pier was not fully repaired until 1921.

In 1971 the pier was declared dangerous, and closed to the public. In 1974 ownership of the pier passed to Arfon Borough Council who decided to demolish it. This provoked a public outcry, the pier was given listed building status, and in 1975 Bangor City Council bought it for a penny. Restoration work began in 1982. The pier was completely reconstructed from end to end. Grants came from the Welsh Development Agency, the National Heritage Memorial Fund, the Historic Buildings Council for Wales, the Manpower Services Commission, a public appeal and the City of Bangor Council. The work was carried out by the Community Task Force, Alfred McAlpine Management Ltd. and L G Mouchell & Partners.

It was a proud day on 7 May 1988 when the Marquis of Anglesey and Lord Lieutenant of Gwynedd officially re-opened Bangor Garth Pier. The pier, quite rightfully, was given a British construction industry award.

Bangor Garth Pier, 1904 (Tim Mickleburgh collection)

CHRIS'S VERDICT: a gem, almost perfect
WALK TIME: 4 min 21 sec

Status: Grade II*
Work started: 1893
First opened: 14 May 1896, re-opened 7 May 1988
Designer: John James Webster, London
Contractor: A Thorne
Construction: cast iron screw piles concreted into well holes supporting steel lattice girders; timber joists; planked decking
Original length: 1550 ft (473 m)
Present length: 1500 ft (458 m)
Ship collision: 1914
Restoration: 1914, 1982–1988
Present owners: Bangor City Council
Website: www.bangorcivicsociety.org.uk

BEAUMARIS

Fine gates at the pier entrance (author's collection)

ANGLESEY'S ONLY SEASIDE PIER

One good reason to visit Anglesey – apart from going on Beaumaris Pier – is that you get to cross the Menai Strait by one of its two magnificent bridges. Thomas Telford's suspension road bridge was opened on 30 January 1826 to great fanfare. It reduced travelling time from London to Holyhead from 36 hours to 27 hours. Robert Stephenson's Britannia railway bridge was opened on 5 March 1850. It was rebuilt after a disastrous fire in 1970 and now carries both rail and road traffic. The Liverpool & North Wales Steamship Co. ran services from Beaumaris pier to Menai Bridge, Llandudno and Liverpool.

A 300-feet pier built on wooden piles was opened in 1846, but suffered storm damage and was not rebuilt until 1872. In 1895 Beaumaris Pier was extended to 570 feet (174 metres) and was later described as 'the new pleasure pier'. A 30-inch gauge baggage line was also added. Previous to that, passengers' bags had to be carried or trollied along the length of the pier. Mineral wagons were also pushed along the line. A sea-end pavilion was added, but that went in the 1950s when the T-head became dangerous and was demolished. Since then the pier has been repaired regularly and is in good nick. In the 1960s Beaumaris Town Council did £15,000-worth of restoration work on the pier, which was passed on to the Isle of Anglesey Borough Council in 1974. Extensive repairs were made in 1987, and there has been regular maintenance since.

The main part of the pier is a solid stone causeway, with only a short length on wooden trestles leading to the pier head, where there are seats all round and a very good shelter with compartments on all four sides, so you can avoid the wind and rain from whichever quarter. The two small side gates at the pier entrance are a joy, and there is a modern paddling pool at the back of the lifeboat station alongside the pier. Crab fishing and trips to Puffin Island are advertised at the small entrance shop. And, there are great views of Snowdonia across the Menai Strait. But once again a pleasant pier is spoiled by those horrible black litter bins!

Beaumaris Pier, c.1906 (Frances Foote collection)

Beaumaris Pier, 2007 (author's collection)

CHRIS'S VERDICT: short and squat, but you can learn to love it
WALK TIME: 1 min 36 sec

Work started: 1845
First opened: 1846
Designer: Frederick Foster (his only pier)
Construction: originally iron girders on wooden piles; now part in stonework (shoreward end) and timber and ironwork (seaward end)
Original length: 570 ft (174 m)
Present length: 570 ft (174 m)
Restoration: 1872, 1895, 1960s, 1970s, 1987 – present
Present owners: Isle of Anglesey Borough Council
Website: www.beaumaris.org.uk

BLACKPOOL CENTRAL

Blackpool Central – the big wheel was soon back on its stand (author's collection)

'THE PEOPLE'S PIER'

Some piers are famous for their looks, and some for their views, but Blackpool's Central Pier was built for fun – and it's for fun rather than fresh air that hundreds of thousands of holidaymakers get on board every year. That is, unless you count the views from the pier's 108-foot-high Ferris wheel, now known as the Blackpool Eye and a major attraction in its own right. You can still see signs of the Central Pier's Victorian origins … but it's fun for the most part. With the big wheel and the Legends Show Bar, the Central Pier is one of Blackpool's premier family destinations.

The big wheel is 108 feet (33 metres) tall and carries 216 passengers. It opened on Good Friday, 1990, at £1 a ride. Including strengthening the pier, the total cost was £750,000.

The pier's shore-side pavilion is bold and brash and more than holds its own on Blackpool's Golden Mile. It promises – and delivers – 'family fun above the sea'. On my visit, the sea-end pavilion was about to get a much-needed facelift for the 2008 season. Much of the original seating around the pier head and along the deck is well-maintained. There are tables and chairs beside the Pier End Bar, and telescopes. There is plenty of room to walk on both sides.

The Central Pier – originally called the South Pier – opened for business in 1868, five years after its close companion the North Pier. In fact, the pier company was headed by the same Major Francis Preston who had master-minded the building of the North Pier some five years earlier. Six of the eleven North Pier directors came with him. The first pile was driven on 3 July 1867, and the completed pier was opened on 30 May 1868. In contrast to the North Pier, there was no public ceremony. The Central Pier was not a success until Robert Bickerstaffe, former coxswain of the first Blackpool lifeboat and a local hero, was appointed as manager in 1870.

On his first day in charge, 'Young Bob' counted only thirteen visitors on *his* pier. He resolved to change all that. Bob organised a cheap steamer trip to Southport at 1s. per head instead of the usual

2s. He had handbills printed, and put them round the town himself. With 250 paying customers, Bob had to find something to entertain them and quickly hired a 'German Band'. On returning from their steamer trip, some of the passengers spontaneously started to dance to the band on the pier deck. Some stayed until the early hours. Open-air dancing on the pier had arrived, and Young Bob had a success on his hands. 'Two Quadrille Bands play for dancing on the pier head and centre platform, open-air concerts, daily Central Pier Collegians entertainment,' said the adverts. The bands played polkas, lancers and quadrilles. In 1873 a band was paid £3 10s. for a six-day week, extra for Sundays. Their income was augmented by passing round the collection plate. In 1886 a nine-piece band got £12 7s. 6d. for the week, with no collections. To accommodate the burgeoning steamer business, some excursions started as early as 5.30 a.m.! Steamer excursions ran from the pier head, to Morecambe, Barrow, Lytham, Liverpool and Llandudno. In

Bob Bickerstaff had distinguished himself on a cold November night in 1862 when he swam out to a wrecked ship, trailing a rope behind him – a terrific feat. All but one of the crew of the schooner *Ada* were rescued, although Bob himself was said to be 'almost dead' when he was finally pulled ashore. When the brig *Favourite* ran aground off Cleveleys on a wild November night in 1865. 'Young Bob' tried for two hours to get to the doomed ship, but was beaten back by the waves. Sadly, all the crew of the *Favourite* were drowned. In February 1880 the schooner *Bessie Jones* was wrecked on Salthouse Bank in a northwesterly gale. One of the crew had already been swept to his death; the rest lashed themselves to the rigging. Again Bob Bickerstaff had his lifeboat out for two hours before getting them ashore at St Anne's beach. Six years later came the *Mexico* disaster at St Anne's. (q.v.)

Blackpool Central's crowded beach (courtesy of Six Piers)

Blackpool Central's entrance, c.1890 (courtesy of Six Piers)

Donkey shelter under the old lifeboat house
(author's collection)

1891 a 400-foot low-water jetty was added to make the overall length of the pier 1,518 feet The jetty, used for angling and boat trips, was demolished 1976, reducing the length of the pier to 1,118 feet (339 metres).

Blackpool's second oldest pier had to change its name from South to Central when the Victoria Pier was opened by the South Shore in 1893. The Central Pier earned its title as 'The People's Pier' when it became popular for its open-air dancing, frowned upon by the more *posh* people frequenting the more sedate North Pier who thought it 'lowered the tone'. Open-air dancing – protected by screens – reached a peak in the 1930s. It declined gradually after World War II, and finished altogether in the 1960s. In 1967 the pier head dance area became the New Theatre, and dancing was moved indoors to the White Pavilion, originally built in 1903.

In 1909, a roller-skating rink opened. The admission fee was one halfpenny. In 1911 the Joy Wheel was introduced, and in 1920 speedboats and racing car rides. An advertising card promoting roller-skating, *c*.1915, reads: 'Invigorating, fascinating, open-air skating! Unrivalled 'Firmit' skating surface, Central Pier Blackpool.' 1932 saw a Guess-Your-Weight machine, a photograph booth and, believe it or not, an automatic chip dispenser. Swimming races between the North and Central piers provided more open-air entertainment. In 1933 the Central Pier Theatre, built as a replica of the Taj Mahal, burned down. The centre platform, used for open-air dancing, became an open-air theatre in 1949. In 1967 the pier front was rebuilt. It had previously been altered in 1877 and 1903.

Storm damage in 1964 reduced the length of the pier, and in 1976 the remaining jetty was blown up. After a fire destroyed the White Pavilion in 1966, its replacement the Dixieland Pal-

Crowded promenade and beach, Central Pier, c.1930 (courtesy of Northern Writers)

Happy al fresco roller-skaters, Central Pier, c.1910
(courtesy of Northern Writers)

Blackpool Central Gay Nineties programme
(courtesy of Six Piers)

ace, was built in only ten weeks at a cost of £150,000. Another fire there in 1973 saw 1,500 people evacuated safely. The Palace had to be rebuilt. When the Ferris wheel was installed in 1990 the pier had to be strengthened and the total cost was around £750,000. The pier end theatre, modernised in 1986 at a cost of £400,000 as *Maggie May's*, became *Peggy Sue's Showboat* and is now the Family Bar hosting live family entertainment nightly. At the shore end, the old Dixieland Palace now houses an amusement arcade and a nightclub, the famous Legends Show Bar.

There are also dodgems, waltzers and ten-pin bowling, and walkways on both sides from the promenade.

CHRIS'S VERDICT: good fun!
WALK TIME: 3 min 33 sec

Work started: July 1867
First opened: 30 May 1868
Designer: J I Mawson (his only pier)
Contractor: R Laidlaw & Sons, Glasgow
Construction: cast iron columns, wrought iron girders; cast iron trestles under a wooden deck
Original length 1518 ft (463 m)
Present length: 1118 ft (341 m)
Fire: 1973
Restoration: 1877, 1903, 1966/7, 1973/4, 1978, 1986, 1990
Legal: Blackpool South Pier Orders 1866–1920
Original owners: The Blackpool South Jetty Co.
Present owners: Six Piers Ltd.
Website: www.visitnorthwest.com/blackpool/central-pier

BLACKPOOL NORTH

Sun worship on North Pier, c.1950 (courtesy of Northern Writers)

BLACKPOOL'S TOP SUNBATHING SPOT

Blackpool's Grade II listed North Pier, voted 'Pier of the Year' in 2004, is the longest and the most traditional of the resort's three piers. Much of its original ornate Victorian design still survives. The North Pier was very much aimed to attract the more genteel classes. There were no amusement arcades until 1960s, but it did provide an impressive 3,000 deckchairs. As a small boy on holiday I remember my 'posh' grandmother insisting that we could only go on the North Pier, as the other two piers were 'common'.

Today you are charged fifty-pence admission for 'the best views in Blackpool' and a free ride on the carousel. You're invited to take a stroll down 402 metres of decking and travel back in style on the North Pier Tram. Is the North Pier longer than Blackpool Tower is tall? The Tower is 518 feet, 9 inches (158 metres) tall, whereas the North Pier is more than two and a half times longer at 1,318 feet (402 metres).

The Talking Telescope (50 pence a view or £1 for longer) at the end of the pier points you to the Isle of Man, Barrow-in-Furness, the Lake District, Morecambe Bay, Snowdonia and the North Wales coast – depending on the weather, of course. Both the Pier Theatre and the Carousel Bar offer entertainment at the end of the pier, if not the traditional 'end of the pier' show of yesteryear.

On entering this well-maintained pier, there is a blue plaque commemorating an important event that took place here on 19 July 1948. That was the day and this was the place where Harry Corbett (not to be confused with Harry H Corbett of *Steptoe & Son* fame) discovered Sooty, possibly the most endearing and best-recognised glove puppet of all time. It's next to the notice about 'Private Fishing only'. Harry Corbett bought Sooty from a stall on the pier for a few shillings, to amuse his children on rainy days during their holiday. By coincidence, *The Sooty Show* ('come and see everyone's favourite yellow bear') was playing on the North Pier from September to October 2007. Down the slope at the side as you enter the pier – watch out for the bump near the bottom!

The North Pier has a broad, spacious deck, with seats on both sides. There are no seats on the station platform, but you can lounge under the station canopy while waiting for the pier train, or not, as the case may be. Now where can you do that on any normal railway station in the country? Along the deck are four miniature, octagonal Moorish 'onion dome' pavilions with fancy weather boarding under the roof: a delicious confection, and I'm not just talking about the ice cream! There's a slight slope down to the pier head with its 35-foot carousel, bar and extensive glass-walled shelter, and loungers on the pier head.

Blackpool's North Pier is the place to go for sunbathing, fresh air and sea views. All along the pier deck are chairs, deckchairs and loungers, at no extra charge. There are canopies and sun lounges, the biggest and best being the Carousel Lounge. Completely enclosed by its glass walls but open to the sky, you can sit, read, take in the entertainment or just sleep – enjoying the sun and the views while protected from what can be a cold wind even in summer.

The North Pier entertainments include an amusement arcade, coffee shop and Gipsy Sarah Petrulengo. Young children can enjoy a ride on the traditional hobby horse carousel and a trip on the pier tram, installed as recently as 1991. This pier is ideal for older folk and indeed for anyone who wants a quiet time with entertainment to hand. It's definitely not for boisterous teenagers or fun-loving adults on the spree – but Blackpool offers almost unlimited scope for such people on its other two piers, and on the Golden Mile and South Shore Pleasure Beach.

Blackpool's North Pier is the oldest surviving seaside pier designed by the great Victorian engineer Eugenius Birch. A meeting in the town's Clifton Hotel on 31 December 1861 led to the formation of the Blackpool Pier Co. Ltd. the following year; twenty businessmen investing a total of £12,000 in the project. It actually cost £13,500. When the first pile was screwed into the seabed on 27 June 1862, company chairman Major Francis Preston declared it would grow into 'one of the most amazing aggregations of public amusements in the world'. He was not far wrong. By 1898 each of the company's £5 shares was worth £275, an increase of 5,400 per cent! Attendances were 275,000 in the first year, 400,000 the next year and 465,000 in 1865. In 1866 the pier took £2,800 in income for an expenditure of £800. In its early years the pier company rarely paid a dividend of less than 12 per cent.

Twenty thousand people turned up for the official opening on 21 May 1863. First there was a 'grand procession' through the town, headed by the town crier. The streets were decorated with flags and bunting, there were several brass

The two-ton carousel was put in place in June 1991. It is 35 feet in diameter, and carries 70 passengers. The 36-inch single-track North Pier tramway, 250 metres long, opened on Monday, 2 September 1991. For the technical-minded, it's driven by a 2.3 litre Perkins diesel, with three single-deck bogie cars.

Blackpool Tower from the North Pier, c.1910 (Frances Foote collection)

Blackpool North, c.1890 (courtesy of Six Piers)

Blackpool North's entrance, c.1900 (courtesy of Six Piers)

bands, plus Major Preston's 12-pound cannon. Marching in the procession were The Volunteer Artillery, Deputations of Freemasons, Oddfellows, Board of Health, Manchester City Band, The Trades of Blackpool: the Butchers, the Joiners, the Painters, the Printers, the Boatmen with a mounted boat, the Blacksmiths, the Stonemasons, the Shrimpers, the Fire Engine, Juvenile Brass Band of the Manchester Ragged and Industrial Schools, Ancient Order of Druids (with two High Priests in full costume, and a Bard mounted on an ass), Independent Order of Mechanics, the Bathing Vans, the Hackney Carriages, the Donkeys, the Chimney Sweep, and, last but not least, 'the multitude'. After Major Preston had performed the opening ceremony, 150 sat down to a ceremonial dinner at the Clifton Hotel. The grand opening made the cover of the *Illustrated London News* with an engraving, no less. The *Illustrated London News* supplement (yes, they had supplements in those days too!) of 20 May 1863 announced: 'Opening of the new pier at Blackpool, Lancashire.' The picture shows the procession retuning to the pier. In 'A Grand day for Blackpool', bands played *The Blackpool Pier Polka*.

Promenaders were charged two-pence admission. For this they could enjoy the seats, shelters, refreshment stalls and lighting. Unlike its soon-to-be rival, the Central Pier, the North Pier did not allow dancing, and 'comic singing' was frowned upon. So, no karaoke, then. Many of the spectators had come by train, the pier being conveniently situated close to the town's newly-opened railway station at the other end of Talbot Road. The pier company ran two pleasure steamers which took trippers to Southport, Liverpool, Llandudno, the Isle of Man and the Lake District.

The pier was 28 feet wide, with 12,000 tons of metal in its construction. A low-water jetty was added in 1866, and extended three years later to bring the overall length of the pier to 1,650 feet (503 metres). In 1874 the north wing was added and the 2,000-seater Indian Pavilion built, along with a bandstand, a restaurant and shops, extending the deck area of the pier by an additional 5,000 square yards. This pavilion was based on the Temple of Binderaband in India. The south wing was added to the pier head in 1877 and electric lighting installed.

OPENING OF THE NEW PIER AT BLACKPOOL, LANCASHIRE: THE PROCESSION RETURNING FROM THE PIER —SEE NEXT PAGE.

Blackpool North opening, 1863 (from Illustrated London News, *courtesy of Six Piers)*

In 1896 the pier neck was widened to almost twice its original size, and in 1903 a new theatre was built. The Indian Pavilion, opened in 1874, burned down in a fire on 11 September 1921. The wreckage was sold for scrap for £310, and the pavilion rebuilt. The old pavilion had featured concerts by the distinguished flautist Edward de Jong who conducted the Pier Orchestra. Later conductors included Simon Spellman, who was to find fame with the Manchester Halle Orchestra, and the fondly-remembered 'Toni' with his shock of hair. A new pavilion, seating 1,500, was built in 1923. In 1932 a sun lounge replaced the bandstand, and in 1938 a café was added. On the evening of 19 June 1938, there was a huge blaze at the sea-end Pier Pavilion. 'Pillars of fire and smoke from the blazing structure mounted to a height of hundreds of feet. The conflagration was watched by a crowd of over 200,000 holidaymakers,' said a local report. The new pavilion was destroyed by the fire, but another new one was built the same year, seating 1,564 people. In 1985 singer Vince Hill spotted smoke coming from the theatre as he left the North Pier after his show. Hill raised the alarm and helped fight the fire.

North Pier on fire, 19 June 1938 (courtesy of Northern Writers)

Blackpool North – paddle steamer, c.1865 (courtesy of Six Piers)

Nelson's former flagship the *Foudreyant*, a 2,055-ton warship of 80 guns built in 1798, came to Blackpool in 1897. On 15 June there was a dance on board, but a gale on the 16 saw the crew of 28 men and boys in peril as the ship, which had been moored to the pier, broke anchor. The *Foudreyant* just missed the North Pier.

The landing jetty had to be closed in 1987 because of storm damage, and it was four years before it re-opened, with helicopter flights as an added attraction. The pier entrance buildings were rebuilt in 1989 at a cost of £350,000. Ship excursions re-started from the pier in 1992 with the arrival of MV *Balmoral*. A severe storm on Christmas Eve 1997 closed the jetty and severed the landing jetty from the rest of the pier. Later storms in January 1998 caused £1.3 million-worth of damage.

The North Pier has twice suffered from ship collision, first in 1892. On the morning of Sunday, 9 October 1892, a hurricane sent giant waves crashing over the prom. The 667-ton Norwegian barque *Sirene* was driven into the pier by the raging storm, destroying six shops. The crew were able to scramble up onto the pier to safety. Next day people crowded onto the beach to help themselves to furs and costume jewellery that had spilled onto the sands from the wrecked ship – shades of the looting of the MSC *Napoli* when she was wrecked off the Devon coast in 2007. No lives were lost. In 1894, The Norwegian ship *Abana*, a 1,269-ton barque under Capt Danielsen, foundered at Norbreck, close to the shore. Unable to launch close by, the Blackpool lifeboat was taken on a horse-drawn cart to Bispham and launched from there. Cox Cartmel took all the crew on board his lifeboat and he and his men rowed back to shore. At one point the lifeboat got stuck on a sandbank, but some of the men jumped out, pushed the boat off, and jumped back in, to get everyone to safety.

The North Pier has always provided top-class entertainment. Lawrence Wright, founder of the *Melody Maker* music magazine, produced *On with the Show*! on the North Pier from 1924–1956. His stars included Frank Randle, Albert Modley, 'two-ton' Tessie O'Shea, the Tiller Girls, the Beverley Sisters and Frankie Vaughan. Bernard Delfont presented *Showtime* from 1957–1983. He brought in Tommy Cooper, the Hollies, Paul Daniels, the Krankies, Lenny Henry and the Black Abbotts. 1971 the diminutive Jimmy Clitheroe ('the Clitheroe Kid') topped the bill with pop group *Freddie and the Dreamers*. Bobby Crush has appeared, and in 1986 Russ Abbott played to a total of half a million people on the North Pier, taking £2 million at the box office – a pier record!

Blackpool's North Pier is the most traditional of Blackpool's three piers, and – thanks to continuing renovation by pier owners Six Piers – it still has much of its original Victorian charm.

Blackpool North – pier head aerial view, 1936 (courtesy of Six Piers)

Pier head station, North Pier (author's collection)

Although the North Pier is not as brash as its two neighbours, being ideal for promenading and sunbathing, it still has its racy side. There's adult comedy in the Merrie England Bar, 'not for the easily offended'. The star entertainer is comic Joey Blower, who just happens to own nearby Fleetwood Pier!

CHRIS'S VERDICT: classic Victorian pier
WALK TIME: 4 min 07 sec

Status: Grade II
Work started: 27 June 1862
First opened: 21 May 1863
Designer: Eugenius Birch
Contractor: R Laidlaw
Construction: cast iron and wrought iron piles spanned by plate girders under a wooden deck
Original length: (i) 1410 ft (430 m); (ii) 1869: 1650 ft (503 m)
Present length: 1318 ft (402 m)
Storm damage: 1987, 1997
Ship collisions: 1892, 1897
Fire: 1921, 1938, 1985
Restoration: 1870, 1980, 1991
Legal: Blackpool Pier Act & Orders 1863–1920
Original owners: The Blackpool Pier Co. Ltd.
Present owners: Six Piers Ltd.
Pier of the Year: 2004
Website: www.visitnorthwest.com/blackpool/north-pier

BLACKPOOL SOUTH

South Pier front during renovation (author's collection)

DEVOTED TO FUN

Entirely devoted to fun, Blackpool South Pier – originally the Victoria Pier – is some distance from the town's other two piers. Close to the Pleasure Beach with its huge funfair, big dipper and other 'white-knuckle' rides, it is the most down-to-earth of the three. At the time of writing, Blackpool South Pier is having a major refurbishment. 'We are remodelling – thank you for your patience' reads the sign.

Indeed there's a whole lot of fun to be had here. The pier has its own funfair and amusement arcade, and there is Carmen Petrulengo to tell your fortune. There is private fishing at the end of the pier. Most spectacular is the pier end bungee jump for those brave souls who not only want to leap off a platform from a great height, but also get a kick out of swinging way out over the sea. There are two amusement arcades, a family bar, dodgems and a Skycoaster® ride. You can 'promenade' along the pier which has a walkway from the prom on both sides.

Renamed the South Pier in 1930, it was as the Victoria that Blackpool's third pier was opened on Good Friday, 31 March 1893. It was 492 feet long, cost £50,000, and had no fewer than 36 shops, shelters and a pavilion. To entertain the crowds that day, there was a 40-piece orchestra, two brass bands and a choir. There were 12,000 visitors on the first day, and 13,000 on the Easter Monday. The Blackpool South Shore & Pavilion Co. had been formed in 1890. The Grand Pavilion, which opened on 20 May 1893 and originally featured a permanent 40-piece orchestra, was damaged by fires in 1954 and 1958 but survived, despite the latter causing £100,000 of damage. It was then altogether destroyed by fire in 1964, only to be completely rebuilt as the Rainbow Theatre in just twelve weeks at a cost of £90,000. It was finally demolished in 1998 to make way for the pier's white-knuckle rides. The 1,300-seat Regal Theatre, built at the shore end in 1937 when the original entrance pavilion was demolished, became the Beachcomber Amusement Arcade in 1963.

In 1968 the pier was taken over by Trust House Forte. Theatre acts included *Freddie & the Dreamers*, Hylda Baker and Tom O'Connor. The actor John Inman, best known for his catchphrase 'I'm free!' in the television comedy series *Are you being served?* made his professional debut on Blackpool South Pier in 1948, aged 13. He died in March 2007.

A storm in 1990 caused a twelve-foot gap to appear across the pier entrance.

The whole of Blackpool's South Shore is being refurbished in a multi-million pound scheme to give new life to a promenade that had been showing its age. There is already a seaside walk and cycleway along to the next resort of St Anne's, starting at the South Pier. With its telescopes, the South Pier claims to have the 'best sea views in Blackpool' – debateable, unless you count the views from the top of the various 'amusements' at the end of the pier that fling you out, up and over the sea – all in good fun, of course.

Blackpool South Pier theatre, 24 March 1896 (courtesy of Six Piers)

Blackpool South programme, 1938 (courtesy of Six Piers)

CHRIS'S VERDICT: Fun, fun, fun!

WALK TIME: 3 min 15 sec

Work started: 1892
First opened: 1893
Designer: T P Worthington & J D Harker (their only pier)
Contractor: J Butler & Co., Leeds
Construction: iron piers, steel decking
Original length 492 ft (150 m)
Present length: 492 ft (150 m)
Storm damage: 1990
Fire: 1954, 1958, 1964
Restoration: 1959, 1963/4
Legal: Blackpool South Shore Pier Orders 1891 & 1924
Original owners: Blackpool South Shore & Pavilion Co.
Present owners: Six Piers Ltd.
Website: www.visitnorthwest.com/blackpool/spouth-pier

BOGNOR REGIS

Promenade and pier, c.1929 (Frances Foote collection)

HOME OF THE ORIGINAL BIRDMAN RALLY

This is a plain pier, with nothing added, behind a handsome front pavilion, unusually entitled the Conservatory. The Conservatory encloses a gift shop, an amusement arcade, a nightclub and a snooker club. Palmist Gypsy Lee has to make do with a hut next to the toilets across the road. There is fishing from the pier.

Most people can bring to mind the Birdman Rally, which involves all kinds of people with all kinds of wings and various 'flying' contraptions jumping off the end of the pier, competing for a £25,000 prize. The Birdman Rally is held at high tide, which is perhaps just as well. The 2007 Birdman competition was won by Ron Freeman of Newbiggin-by-the-Sea., joint winner in 2006. There were 'official' birdman entries from Bulgaria, Holland and the USA.

At other times 'divers and jumpers' are strictly prohibited. On 24 August 2005, a 16-year-old youth was seriously injured after jumping off the pier. Fifteen years older than its rival competition at Eastbourne, the Bognor Birdman contest was fantastic fun for spectators and participants alike, and it couldn't be more British. This is how we show the world just how eccentric we can be. Remember, we are also the nation that created the Mulberry Harbour. Sadly, in March 2008, 60 feet of decking was removed on safety grounds. The Birdman Rally was cancelled as the water was too shallow.

Bognor Regis Pier has suffered a lot in the last forty-odd years. A huge storm on 3 March 1965 sent the far end section of the pier crashing into the sea. It had already suffered storm damage the previous year. Apart from the shore end, the pier fell into disuse. The pier was then sold for £35,000, but after two serious fires within the space of three months, it was closed in December 1974. By 1992 the pier was in such bad condition it was estimated to need at least £500,000 to restore it. Two years later came the inevitable application to demolish this queen – or rather plain princess – of piers. New owners took over in 1995 and 1996, but their efforts to obtain grant funding were in vain. Now the pier survives with only its shore-end facilities to keep it going.

Built in 1864/5 as promenade pier a thousand feet long, Bognor Regis was the first pier designed by Joseph William Wilson, in conjunction with Sir Charles Fox, and had first been planned as long ago as 1835. It was opened on 5 May 1865. The local Board bought the pier in 1876 for £1,200. A small bandstand was added in 1880, a pavilion at the sea end in 1900, and a small landing stage in 1903. When Bognor Urban District Council, successors to the Board, found that they could not afford to pay for necessary repairs, they sold the pier to private owners in 1909. The new owners spent £30,000 widening the deck to 80 feet and building a new entertainment complex at the shore end. This was comprised of a cinema, theatre, a roof garden restaurant and an arcade. All this opened for business on August Bank Holiday, 1912.

Bognor Regis Pier saw service in two world wars. During World War I, 200 men were billeted there. In World War II, the pier was taken over by the Royal Navy as HMS *Patricia*.

Bognor Regis Pier, c.1933
(courtesy of the National Piers Society)

Bathing machines on Bognor beach, c.1908
(Frances Foote collection)

Bognor Regis Pier – straight and simple pier deck
(author's collection)

CHRIS'S VERDICT: plain and simple
WALK TIME: 1 min 35 sec

Status: Grade II
Work started: 1864
First opened: 5 May 1865
Designer: Joseph William Wilson, Sir Charles Fox
Construction: cast iron trestles under a wooden deck (?)
Original length 1000 ft (305 m)
Present length: 350 ft (107 m)
Landing stage: 1903
Storm damage: 1964, 1965
Fire: 1974
Restoration: 1910–12
Original owners:
Present owners: Bognor Pier Leisure Ltd.
Website: www.bognor-regis.co.uk

BOSCOMBE

Paddle steamer approaches Boscombe Pier, 1908 (courtesy of Bournemouth Borough Council)

EUROPE'S FIRST ARTIFICIAL SURF REEF

Boscombe is an outstanding example of what can be achieved by combining the old with the new to create a twenty-first century pier. Not only is Boscombe Pier being completely refurbished, it will be at the very heart of a major resort development that includes Europe's first artificial surf reef (one of only four in the world). The reef – 1,600 feet long – will lie 300 metres east of the pier, and was planned to be completed by the end of 2007. It will be constructed of hundreds of sunken sandbags that will amplify the wave-height by two and a half times. These are no ordinary sandbags; they are 'geotextile' bags up to 30 metres long. The reef will be a haven for marine wildlife. If it works as planned, it should also be a mecca for surfers. And, the best place to watch them will be from the pier.

There will be a piazza and events area in front of the pier, 42 'super chalets' for hire, and a revised Boscombe Overstrand complex of shops and a restaurant. With 169 new one- and two-bedroomed apartments being built at the adjacent Honeycombe Beach by Barratt Homes, the Boscombe Spa Village development is set to be a major tourist destination. Bournemouth Borough Council has gone into partnership with private enterprise to bring this bold scheme to life. And, all this new development is centred around Boscombe's 120-year old pier!

This pier is remarkable in that 'amusements' were banned until 4 June 1960 when people were officially allowed to have fun there for the first time. The £50,000 amusement centre offered bingo, a rifle range, mini tenpin bowling, a haunted house, and – horror of horrors for Boscombe's straight-laced Victorian fathers – gaming machines!

With the success of Bournemouth Pier and plans underway for Southbourne Pier, the people of Boscombe demanded a pier of their own. A pier company was formed in 1886, and the company prospectus in July 1888 announced a capital £15,000. One of the main shareholders was Sir Percy

Shelley, son of the famous poet. Work began driving first pile on 11 October 1888, and local schoolchildren were given a day's holiday to celebrate.

Built to the design of Archibald Smith, who also designed the pier at his home town of Southbourne, Boscombe Pier was officially opened on 31 July 1889 by the Duke of Argyll. The 600-foot-long pier was built with 40 feet spans, had a frame of wrought iron girders and timber decking 32 feet wide. Ten thousand people paid to enter the pier on its first day, generating £40 income. With its lack of amusements perhaps it is no surprise that Boscombe Pier was not a success. In 1904 it was taken over by Bournemouth Corporation who put up buildings at both ends of the pier, plus a steamer landing stage which proved very popular. It cost more than £4,000 to 'overhaul and thoroughly scrape and paint [the pier] in every part'.

By 1921 the landing stages, vital for attracting steamers to the pier, were 'in a ruinous condition'. In 1925 £22,500 was spent on refurbishing the pier and a reinforced, high-alumina concrete pier head was added, extending the pier by 100 feet. The pier re-opened on 29 May 1927. A 650-seat concert auditorium at the sea end featured a removable canvas roof. At night the pier was illuminated with hundreds of fairy lights.

Requisitioned for the war effort in 1940, the last concert performance was given on 3 July of that year. A few days later, the Army blew up a 60-foot section of the pier deck. All the superstructure was removed as an anti-invasion measure. After World War II, much of the damaged pier was left as a rusting skeleton, however, the intact remainder was re-opened to the public.

War-damage compensation was finally granted, allowing reconstruction work to start in 1958. The pier neck was rebuilt in reinforced concrete. In 1961 a 'modern' pier entrance was built in the shape of a delta wing, along with a restaurant and the Mermaid Theatre which never operated as a theatre; it was a roller-skating rink for two years and then became an amusement arcade. Bournemouth Council took over the Mermaid in 1988 when the lease ended. In 1990 the pier head was closed on the grounds of safety concerns, with the neck remaining open. The entire pier was closed in October 2005, but plans were already afoot for something new and radical by the seaside. By 2007 a whole new future for Boscombe Pier was emerging.

Described bluntly as a 'glorified bus shelter', the Mermaid Hall at the sea end has now been removed

Enjoying the sun and sea air on Boscombe Pier, c.1935. With so many lovely ladies around, why does the bloke sitting on the front row, first left, look so miserable?
(Richard Riding collection)

Boscombe Pier still sectioned due to anti-invasion measures, 1948
(courtesy of Bournemouth Borough Council)

Boscombe Pier, c.1907
(courtesy of the National Piers Society)

and will be replaced by a viewing platform. A new T-head is being built, and there will also be a new windbreak, lighting and wooden decking. Boscombe's transformation into a twenty-first century seaside holiday village is underway, and the pier is being completely renovated for its setting as the centre-piece. And, the cherry on the cake is Europe's first artificial surf reef.

CHRIS'S VERDICT: an exciting and innovative new development
WALK TIME: n/a

Status: Grade II
Work started: 11 October 1888
First opened: 31 July 1889
Designer: Archibald Smith
Contractor: E Howell, Waterloo Foundry, Poole
Construction: original wood and iron; reinforced concrete head, 1926; reinforced concrete neck, 1958
Original length: 600 ft (183 m)
Present length: 750 ft (229 m)
Fire: 1974
Restoration: 1924/5, 1927, 1958–60, 2007–09
Legal: Boscombe Pier Order 1903
Original owners: Boscombe Pier Co.
Present owners: Bournemouth Corporation
Support group: Friends of Boscombe Pier
Website: www.bournemouth.gov.uk

BOURNEMOUTH

Bournemouth pier front (author's collection)

IRA TARGET

Bournemouth Pier is possibly the only British seaside pier to be a target of an IRA bombing campaign. On 13 August 1993, six incendiary devices were set in retail outlets in Bournemouth. Some did not go off, but others did and caused some damage. Two small devices were set on the pier: one exploded, but no-one was injured.

There have been three seaside piers in this location at Bournemouth, if you count the 100-foot-long wooden jetty, built by the local Board of Commissioners, which opened for business on 2 August 1856. Five years later, this simple contraption had been destroyed by the elements and was replaced by a 1,000-foot-long wooden pier designed by George Rennie and built at a cost of £3,418. It opened on 17 September 1861, but the wooden piles were attacked by teredo worm and had to be replaced by cast iron ones. A gale in January 1867 swept away the T-head, and in 1876 another storm made the landing stage unfit for steamer landings. It was demolished and a temporary structure built in time for the 1877 season.

Ace pier designer Eugenius Birch was brought in. He drew up plans for a new 838-foot iron pier, costing £21,600. Opened on 11 August 1880, pier number three proved much more durable than its two predecessors and survives to this day. Covered shelters were added in 1885, and the pier was extended in 1894 and 1905. At that time, the tolls collected amounted to £125 a week. Toll collector Thomas Burt was provided with two suits and two hats each year, and a greatcoat every two years.

A new pavilion costing £40,000 and seating for more than a thousand customers was opened on 26 June 1926. World War II saw Bournemouth Pier suffer the same fate as a number of its southern cousins, and it too was breached to prevent invasion by German troops. Repaired after the

Bournemouth entrance c.1910 (courtesy of Six Piers)

war, the pier re-opened to the public in 1946. The pier head was rebuilt in 1950 and, ten years later, a concrete platform was built to carry the new pier theatre. From 1979–81, £1.7 million was spent on a complete rebuilding programme including a leisure complex and a new concrete neck. In 1996 a hugely ambitious plan to build a £13 million 'high-tech' pier bit the dust.

Bournemouth Council has kept this pier in very good condition. It has been re-decked and there have been extensive structural repairs. On 28 July 2004, the Queen and the Duke of Edinburgh visited Bournemouth Pier and met sixty World War II veterans. The royals were presented with a stick of Bournemouth rock.

The pier windbreaks were due to be replaced by the end of 2007 when re-planking was done. The low concrete arches of the unobstructed pier neck are clean and graceful. There are two large pavilions at each end of the pier, which provide outstanding views all round. The pier head has a theatre, amusement arcade, café, bar, tables and deckchairs for relaxing inside and out. Toll: 50 pence for adults and 30 pence for children

A swarm of 20,000 bees (how do they know how many?) landed on the pier in May 2007, but caused no interference to holidaymakers!

Shows at the Pier Theatre have included Ted Rogers in *Carry on Laughing* {1960}, Thora Hird in *The Best Laid Plans* (1964), Sid James in *Spring Wedding* (1966) Dick Emery in *Oh, You are Awful* (1967), Harry Corbett and Sooty (1968), *The Mating Game* (1969, 1971) and *Rupert Bear* (1975). Barabara Windsor, Terry Scott, June Whitfield, Bobby Davro and Freddie Starr have all appeared at the pier theatre, as well as the television casts of *Hi-de-Hi*, *It Ain't Half Hot Mum* and *Allo, Allo*. The stage comedy *No Sex Please, We're British*, made its national debut at Bournemouth Pier Theatre in 1973. Remarkably, it returned here for a revival in 2000. These shows are typical of many such entertainments on Britain's piers, then and now.

From the air, c.1930
(Frances Foote collection)

Strolling, c.1928
(Frances Foote collection)

Sitting on the pier,
28 August 1924
(Frances Foote collection)

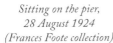

CHRIS'S VERDICT: well-kept pier for quiet enjoyment
WALK TIME: 2 min 55 sec

Work started: (i) 1856; (ii) 1861; (iii) 1878
First opened: (i) 2 August 1856; (ii) 17 September 1861; (iii) 11 August 1880
Designer: (i) unknown; (ii) George Rennie (his one pier); (iii) Eugenius Birch
Construction: (i) timber; (ii) originally timber, wooden piles replaced by cast iron in 1866; (iii) cast iron, wrought iron. Concrete sub-structure placed in 1960 and 1979–81
Original length: (i) 1000 ft (305 m); (ii) 838 ft (256 m); later extended to 1000 ft (305 m)
Present length: 750 ft (229 m)
Storm damage: 1867, 1876
Restoration: 1946, 1950, 1960, 1979–81, 1997–2007
Legal: Bournemouth Pier Act & Orders 1856–1903
Original owners: Board of Commissioners
Present owners: Bournemouth Corporation
Website: www.bournemouth.gov.uk

BRIGHTON PALACE

Controversy over the name – it's now Brighton Pier (author's collection)

'THE ULTIMATE PLEASURE PIER'

Truly the 'Queen of Piers', the genuinely world-famous Brighton Palace Pier on the Sussex coast exemplifies all that is good about British seaside piers. It still has its original charm and grace, and still provides 'fresh air and fun' for its millions of visitors while continuing to adapt to modern requirements. It was named 'Pier of the Year' in 1998 by the National Piers Society. Three years later the pier was re-named 'Brighton Pier' by its owners, the Gateshead-based Noble Organisation, a decision that the NPS did not agree with. Nobles also caused controversy by objecting to the redevelopment of the derelict Brighton West Pier on the grounds that public money was being used to create a commercial operation.

Noble's reason for the name change was set out by Tony Gibbons, managing director of Noble's leisure division who said: 'Brighton Pier is the name most used by people visiting Brighton, and as we spend a considerable amount of money promoting the pier, and by definition Brighton, we feel that it should be clear and obvious to people that the one remaining structure, and facilities, deserve to be referred to as Brighton's Pier, hence the name change.' If and when Brighton West Pier is reborn, as now seems more than possible, Brighton Pier will no longer be Brighton's only 'live' pier. The 'Palace Pier' has a nice ring to it. Nobles could promote that.

For all its glitz and bravado, you can still see and enjoy Brighton Pier's classic Victorian lines: the pavilions, the fancy railings, the cast iron lighting columns each with an attractive four-globe assembly. There are deckchairs, seats and shelters, bars and cafes, but most of all a huge variety of amusements, from a traditional carousel roundabout to dodgems and gut-wrenching rides. You can have your fortune told or enjoy a massage. In mid-pier you'll find a market-cum-fair under cover. There are echoes of the past with the Palm Court Restaurant. This pier is very well maintained and there is a smooth section of deck, particularly welcome to wheelchair users.

The Marine Palace & Pier Co. was formed in 1886 with the task of replacing Brighton's much-loved but doomed Chain Pier. The Palace Pier was opened on Saturday, 20 May 1899. The public were allowed access between 9 a.m. and 9 p.m. for two-pence admission. With its wide deck, dining room, grillroom, smoking and reading rooms, this was truly a palace built to impress. There was a pier-head pavilion and bathing from the landing stage. It cost the then huge sum of £137,000 and had taken ten years to build – a record.

With the iconic Royal Pavilion just up the road, built as an incredibly ornate and extravagant seaside watering-place for the Prince Regent, later King George IV, the Palace Pier had no choice but to acknowledge its haughty neighbour. This, the pier architect Richard St George Moore did superbly well. His 1901 1,500-seat pier theatre, built as the Oriental Pavilion, was dismantled in 1986. The shore-end pavilion dates back to 1910 when there was also a Winter Gardens mid-pier. The famous pier entrance clock-tower, however, scene of so many trysts and family reunions, was not built until 1930.

The Brighton Marine Palace & Pier Act 1888 allowed for a pier 666 yards (809 metres) long with a 3d. toll. The company was required to remove the old Chain Pier. The first screw pile was set in place, amidst much ceremony, on 7 November 1891. The contractors, Mayoh Bros of Manchester, got to work but quit a year later. The pier company took possession of the site and continued building and in 1892 they bought Chain Pier for £15,000, but in March 1895 the pier company ran out of funds. 1,060 feet (323 metres) of the pier had been completed and £43,000 spent. A second Parliamentary Act in 1893 allowed three more years for the pier to be completed. Even this was not enough, and a third Act, the Brighton & Marine Palace Pier Act of 7 August 1896, allowed another three-year extension. In January 1897 there was a winding-up order in the High Court, but it was stayed.

In 1898 six rectangular side kiosks and a front entrance-porch were built. On the 20 May 1899, Brighton Palace Pier was declared open, despite the fact that it was not fully finished. The Chain Pier which it replaced had finally collapsed in a storm on 4 December 1896 after being closed as unsafe earlier that year. Some of the timber from the old pier smashed against the new pier, inflicting some damage. The Palace Pier was built with cast iron columns and lattice girders, and a hardwood deck. Keruing and Kapur timber was used for the 85 miles of deck planking. The ironwork for the pier was forged at the Phoenix Iron Works in nearby Lewes. Eight iron and steel arches carried illuminations. The pier, covering an area of 2.5 acres, had cost the huge sum of £137,000.

The Brighton Electric Railway had opened on 4 August 1883 with a single track to the old Chain Pier. It was later extended to Black Rock. In 1893 Magnus Volk determined to further extend the service eastwards, despite the difficulties of the terrain. He couldn't afford to tunnel

Palace Pier and new Winter Gardens (built 1910), c.1915 (Frances Foote collection)

Fun! the teacup roundabout (courtesy of the Noble Organisation)

This is what deckchairs are for (courtesy of the Noble Organisation)

Fun! water splash (courtesy of the Noble Organisation)

Fun! the dodgems (courtesy of the Noble Organisation)

through the cliffs or go up and over them, so he developed a curious vehicle that ran on stilts through the sea, with an overhead wire system, looking for all the world like a mobile pier. Work began in June 1894 and the service started two years later. The line terminated at Rottingdean where a 300-foot (92 metres) light steel pier was erected. Described as a combination of electric tramcar, pleasure yacht and section of seaside pier, the car was named *Pioneer*. It weighed 50 tons and carried 150 passengers on two decks. Safety equipment included lifebuoys, fire-buckets and even a lifeboat. The line was badly damaged in storm of 4/5 December 1896. *Pioneer* broke away and ran down line before being capsized by the wind. This unique rail service was closed in January 1901 and the car and rails were sold for scrap.

A shore-end pavilion, incorporating a 1,300-seat bandstand and the Winter Gardens, now the Palace of Fun, opened in 1910, and a low-level landing stage was built at the sea end a year later. This finally completed the original plans twenty years after the first pile was driven. There were dining-rooms, grill-rooms, smoking-rooms and reading-rooms, and a 'a new bathing station, gym and hot & cold showers'. The pier was open from 6am to 6pm. In 1914 the deck around the bandstand was widened and the Palace Pier was said to be 'unequalled by any similar undertaking in the United Kingdom'.

The pier was not sectioned in World War I, but sentries were posted, sandbags piled by the rails and mines wired in place to demolish sections of the pier – all in case of invasion

The 1899 arches, which in 1913 carried 15,000 lamps and 100 arcs, were replaced by a canopy and shelters and, in 1931, the deck on the east side was re-laid. The Giant Pleasure Wheel was installed in 1938, when a new sun-deck was built.

Pier swimming races, including a ladies pier-to-pier race between the Palace and West piers, were popular in the 1930s when maintenance was carried out by a diver in full diving gear, helmet, lead boots, etc. Emperor Haile Selassie, exiled from Ethiopia in 1936 when his country was invaded by Italy under fascist dictator Mussolini, took up residence in the UK. In 1938 he was enjoying the sunshine on Brighton's Palace Pier.

Extended in 1938 but 'sectioned' in 1940, the Palace Pier has managed to avoid most of the disasters that have befallen its unfortunate neighbour, the West Pier. But on Wednesday, 23 May 1940, at the time of Dunkirk, the pier was requisitioned without warning. The theatre audience, already seated for the evening performance of *The First Mrs Fraser*, was ordered out and the patrons given their money back. A centre portion of the pier was immediately blown up. During World War II, German dive bombers made several attempts to destroy the pier but only registered near misses. The Palace Pier re-opened on 6 June 1946.

On Friday, 19 October 1973 there was a huge gale. A 70-ton construction barge broke loose from its moorings and collided with the pier. It smashed 25 piles, and destroyed part of the pier deck, the landing stage and the theatre, by then out of use. The empty theatre was declared unsafe and was closed off. The north-east corner of the theatre block sagged two feet and had to be jacked up. Damage was estimated at £100,000. In 1980 the *Athina B*, on its last voyage, narrowly missed the pier, as did a Red Arrow jet that crashed into the sea just off Brighton.

In 1921 an evening's dancing at the Winter Gardens cost 1s. 6d. In 1922 tickets were advertised at 1s., although that might have been a printing error, as the price was soon raised to 2s. In 1922 a pot of tea with bread & butter in the Winter Gardens tea room cost 6d. Compare 1984 prices with those of 2004: deck chairs 30p (free), ice cream 30/40p, (99p, £1.29), dodgems 50p (£1.50), helter-skelter 20p (£1), candy floss 35p (£1.40/£1.80).

In 1932 Madame Lauri Alwyn, in a fetching one-piece body-suit, gave 'displays of physical culture' with her young lady pupils. In 1933 the Oxford Blazers performed what were described as 'University Follies' – the forerunner of the Footlights Revue, perhaps? Comedian Tommy Trinder made 'em laugh on Brighton Pier in 1935 and in 1936 Trinder was spotted by impresario Jack Hylton and his career took off. Brighton's own Max Miller started as a 'bottler', collecting money for acts on the beach. Actress Binnie Hale performed on the pier in 1937 as did comic Vic Oliver the following year. The Palace Pier Carnival on 8 August 1938, which included a 'bathing belle' contest, attracted 18,332 people through the turnstiles that day.

Brighton Palace Pier was used for early BBC live radio broadcasts. On Monday, 12 July 1937, the 1st Battalion, Oxford and Bucks Light Infantry Band played to the nation via the National Programme, 12 noon to 1.10 p.m. On 2 August 1937, the Band of HM Coldstream Guards filled the same slot. The 2nd Battalion Queens Royal Regiment broadcast on the Regional Programme, 3.15–4 p.m., on Thursday, 10 June 1937. On Tuesday, 5 July 1938, the BBC's John Watt introduced a programme of dance music from Brighton. *Brighton Nights* or *The Brighton & Hove Hour*, from 8.30 p.m., featured both the town's piers and went out to 'Empire listeners' and to the USA. The day before, Bobby Martin and his orchestra had made the first of a series of half-hour dance-music radio programmes from the Hotel Metropole.

There was great excitement on August Bank Holiday Monday, 1937 when American broadcaster Edward R Murrow, grandly titled 'European Director of the Columbia Broadcasting System,' made a 15-minute live broadcast from the Palace Pier. It was 5 p.m. BST, 8 a.m. on the USA west coast. A microphone was set up on the pier deck, and Ed's voice was beamed to (a hopefully impressed) American public via London, Rugby and Wayne (New York). Presumably that was Wayne the town and not Wayne the CBS office boy.

Murrow later gave stirring broadcasts from Britain during World War II, assuring the American people that 'London can take it' during the Blitz. He made over 500 live broadcasts in 1936, more than half from the UK. The Murrow broadcast from Brighton Pier was 'the fulfilment of an eleven-year old dream', according to the Corporation's publicity manager, Mr C C Brown. Murrow explained to the USA: 'This Bank Holiday is the workman's holiday and can best be compared with our Labour Day in America'.

Popular piermaster, captain F C Weeks, told Murrow he had sailed the Golden Gate in San Francisco 'many a time' and had made good friends there.

Perhaps the most moving and compelling story about Brighton Palace Pier is that of Oliver Dalton, a local lad made good who rose to own and run the pier, only to commit suicide at the peak of his success. Dalton's widowed mother kept a boarding house in Brighton, near the old Chain Pier. Born in 1879 and twelve years old when the Palace Pier was completed in 1891, Dalton applied for a job there as timekeeper and was taken on as an office boy, aged 13.

After a spell in the Royal Navy, Dalton volunteered to join the Imperial Yeomanry and went to fight in the Boer War, 1899–1902. After the war, he stayed on in South Africa for a few years, returning to Brighton to set up in business as a bathing-hut proprietor. He gradually built up a considerable business, and branched out into automatic machines. Dalton prospered when fruit machines became popular in the 1920s and 1930s. In 1936 he paid the first of a series of visits to the USA, picking up ideas in Atlantic City. Now on the board of the pier company, Dalton introduced the first 'big wheel' to the pier. He was also a member of Brighton Council, 1929–38, and lived in a large house in the best part of town.

Early one morning, in 1939, the Dalton's cook found him in the gas-filled kitchen. He had gassed himself, the inquest found, 'while the balance of his mind was disturbed, after a year of indifferent health'. He was only sixty. Three years earlier, one of his sons had been killed and his wife injured in a car accident. Another son told the inquest that his father had twice recently been a patient at a Hove nursing home, suffering from a nervous breakdown, and had been back home only a short while prior to his death. The funeral was held on 28 October 1939. Dalton, chairman of the pier company, was described as 'one of the richest and most influential men in the town'.

In the hands of the Noble Organisation, the future of Brighton Pier looks assured. Since buying the pier in 1984, Nobles have spent more than £25 million in improvements and maintenance, which they claim is the largest privately-funded restoration project in the UK. The pier attracted two million visitors in 1934 but only 750,000 in 1983. By 2003 this had risen to four million. In 1983, the annual repair bill was £130,000 but by 2004 it was £850,000. The current annual maintenance budget is over £1,000,000, and Nobles meet this without public subsidy.

In 1984 the previous owners raised the pier toll from 20p to 30p. Entry is now free. Nobles made this decision in 1985 when they also offered the use of deckchairs for free, although fishing from the pier was banned during the summer season. Initially introduced as an experiment, admission and use of deck chairs on the pier still remain free. The pier was made open to the public in the evenings and now opens 9 a.m. to 12 midnight Monday to Thursday, and 9 a.m. to 2 a.m. weekends and Bank Holidays. New gates were built in 1986, and the Palace of Fun was given a new front façade. Prior to 1984, Brighton Pier was not lit at night but now its bright illuminations can be seen for miles around.

In March 1986 the pier theatre was dismantled by the Noble Organisation, who replaced it with an amusement pleasure-dome. The idea was for parts of the theatre to be kept in storage and eventually restored. Despite representations from the theatre trust and other bodies, this now seems unlikely. Nobles are of the opinion that Brighton is well served with modern entertainment facilities and a rebuilt pier theatre would simply not be viable.

In December 1994 work began on widening the pier head by 92 feet (28 metres). Noble's £20 million expansion plans in 1995 never came to fruition, but a Ferris wheel was put up in May 1995. A fire on 4 February 2000 destroyed the ghost train, the log flume and the mini-dodgems. New rides introduced in summer that year included the Wild River water flume, the 50 foot (15m) high 'Crazy Mouse' and 'Turbo' roller-coasters. In September 1996 Brighton Pier was the first in the country to be authorised for weddings.

In 1999 local objections to the introduction of twelve new rides were overruled. Likewise, in 2003 objections to Nobles putting two 40 foot (12 metres) roller-coasters on the pier were overruled after a public inquiry. To accusations of 'tackiness', Nobles responded by saying there had been fruit machines and other amusements on the pier for over a century.

By 2007 the Brighton Pier Ghost Train had been replaced with 'the most up-to-date House of Horror', and two 39-metre high 'thrill rides' had been installed. A new food court opened in 2007 and Horatio's Bar was being refurbished in its traditional form for the 2008 season.

Over the years, Brighton Palace Pier has described itself as 'The Pier of the World' (1913), 'The home of pantomime' (1913), 'the popular rendezvous' (1913), 'the Pier of many shelters – comfort in

Charabanc arrives at Palace Pier, c.1920 (courtesy of the Noble Organisation)

all weathers' (1914), 'Dr Brighton's Sea & Sunshine Tonic' (1933), and 'the finest pier in the world' (1933). Brighton Pier now advertises itself in this way: 'It's so hot, they had to put it in the water!', 'Where your fantasy meets reality', 'So much fun, your feet won't touch the ground', 'Now even more ways to horrify your parents – two new coasters!' Attractions include arcades, takeaways, giant funfair, resident DJ, sideshows, Victoria Bar, Pleasure Dome, Offshore Bar. And you can still take a trip along the shore on 'Volks Electric Railway', although not through the waves!

CHRIS'S VERDICT: is what it claims to be: 'year-round entertainment.'
WALK TIME: 5 min 32 sec

Status: Grade II*
Work started: 7 November 1891
First opened: 20 May 1899 (completed 1901)
Designer: Richard St George Moore
Contractor: Mayoh Bros, Manchester (work taken over by the pier company)
Construction: cast iron columns on screw piles, wrought iron bracing, hardwood deck
Original length: 1,760 ft (537 m)
Present length: 1,760 ft (537 m)
Ship collisions: 1973
Fire: 1974
Restoration: 1938, 1994
Legal: Brighton Marine Palace Pier Acts & Orders 1882–1952
Original owners: Marine Palace & Pier Co.
Present owners: The Noble Organisation
Support group:
Pier of the Year: 1998
Website: www.brightonpier.co.uk

BRIGHTON WEST

*Artist's impression: the **i360** in place (courtesy of Marks Barfield Architects)*

'WALKING ON AIR' –
TWENTY-FIRST CENTURY PIER

Visiting Brighton in 2007, it was difficult to imagine that the gaunt, broken skeleton still defying the sea was to be reborn with a new concept in pier design – the vertical pier. Yet on 11 October 2006, Brighton and Hove Council approved plans to build the 'Brighton **i360**', the highest viewing platform in Europe, at the base of Brighton West Pier which – equally astonishingly – is to be partly rebuilt. So as well as 'walking on water' at the West Pier, you'll be able to 'walk on air' – truly a pier for the twenty-first century.

The people who created the London Eye are behind the 500-foot-high **i360** 'pier-in-the-sky' which they estimate will attract 600,000 visitors a year. Silent wind turbines on the top of the spire will generate 20% of its energy needs. One hundred visitors at a time – carried up in four-metre wide, aerodynamically-designed pods – will have truly outstanding views over the South Downs and the English Channel from the observation deck, which will be four metres taller than the London Eye. Work on the **i360** viewing tower was due to start in Autumn 2007, with a projected completion date of summer 2009. The 'Old Lady' will sport the very latest exclusive accessory, as well as having a completely new outfit. Dr Geoff Lockwood, chief executive of the West Pier Trust describes the plans as a 'stunning proposal, a unique vertical pier in the tradition and spirit of the West Pier'.

Yet the West Pier could so easily have been lost forever. In October 1970 the sea end of the pier was sealed due to being dangerous. Things came to a head in 1974 when the Department of Environment gave listed building consent for the seaward end to be dismantled. A 'We-Want-the-West-Pier' campaign was started by local resident John Lloyd, and the same year the Brighton West Pier Trust was formed. In 1975 the whole of the pier was declared unsafe and closed to the public on 30 September. In 1984 the West Pier Trust bought the pier for a nominal £100. After particularly severe storms in 1987 and 1988, a 110-foot section had to be removed, leaving the Concert Hall and Pavilion stranded. There seemed to be hope in 1996 with the award of a £1 million grant from the Heritage Lottery Fund. A steel walkway was built to reconnect the Concert Hall and Pavilion with the shore end. A further £14 million was made available in 1998.

After years of effort, everything was in place to rebuild the pier when it was hit by a series of disasters. Severe storms on 29 December 2002 and 20 January 2003 caused a partial collapse of the pier and the concert hall. Worse was to follow with two arson attacks. On the morning of Friday, 28 March 2003 a huge fire started at the pier-head pavilion. The blaze destroyed the building and raged through the remaining sections of the pier. Due to the partial collapse of the pier the year before, it was impossible for the fire crews to reach the burning building from land, and they had to operate from small boats. Even this had to end by 3 p.m. due to the fading light and the state of the tide.

A second arson attack, less than two months later, on 10 May 2003, started a fire in the mid-pier Concert Hall which, although damaged by storms that winter, was still standing and intact. This fire was fought by firefighters from inside the building until it became unsafe for them to continue and they were forced to withdraw. This fire left the Concert Hall as a shell. Another destructive storm hit on 23 June 2004 and it collapsed into the sea. All that remained were the bare bones of the West Pier's iron frame – which was then further twisted and broken by the violent sea.

But the Brighton West Pier Trust, which has an office at the pier base, showed remarkable resilience. The Trust did its best to keep the funding organisations on board, but first the Heritage Lottery Fund and then English Heritage withdrew their support. However, the Trust did not give up, and their joint plans with Marks Barfield Architects have now been set in motion. The next target for the Trust was to finalise negotiations with a consortium to build a brand new pier in place of the old West Pier.

Looking at the sad remains of Brighton's West Pier in 2007, one can only imagine what it was like in its heyday. Opened in 1866, and know as the 'Pier of the Realm', this was Britain's first Grade I listed seaside pier. There is a little wrinkle to this. The twisted wreckage lying on the seabed is still Grade I listed and so cannot be moved. In order to recover these pier parts and restore them, first they will have to be de-listed. The wonders of regulation and bureaucracy!

Opened on 5 October 1866, designed by Eugenius Birch and built by Laidlaw & Son of Glasgow, Brighton West Pier – 'the Queen of Piers' – cost £30,000. The deck was 55 feet wide, the pier

Brighton West Pier, c.1949 (Frances Foote collection)

Pavilion fire, 28 March 2003 (courtesy of Andrew Dixon Associates)

was 265 feet wide at the land end, and 140 feet at the head. It took three and a half years to build, from April 1863 to October 1866. It was built mainly for promenading, and had an open deck with ramps for bath chairs. There were six ornamental houses, each topped by a small minaret. The toll was 2*d*. (1*d*. on Sundays.) There were benches to seat 2,000–3,000. The pier company operated a strict dress code for promenaders, but 'gentlemen' were allowed to bathe naked from the pier head. In the 1890s the Barrington Foote Concert and Operetta Co. held sway as pier entertainment.

In 1875 600,000 people a year were passing through the turnstiles. For years the pier company was able to declare dividends of up to 12%. In 1893 the pier was extended and a pavilion was built, and the latter enlarged two years later. R W Peregrine Birch, nephew of Eugenius, was the civil engineer in charge. Landing stages were added in 1896. A violent storm on the night of 4 December 1896 washed away the remains of Brighton's old Chain Pier and some of the debris cut the West Pier in two.

The landing stages were extended in 1901. The same year saw the conversion of the pier-head pavilion into a theatre and two games saloons. King Edward VII visited the pier. A Concert Hall replaced the mid-pier bandstand in 1916 when this part of the deck was widened, and a new top-deck entrance was added in 1932. There were over two million paying customers in 1919/20. The pier still had an open deck in the 1930s, when men were still allowed to bathe naked. However, by the start of World War II numbers of visitors to the pier had fallen to 760,000, despite the introduction of a fun fair and other amusements.

The West Pier will rise again. Gaunt remains in 2007 (author's collection)

From the turn of the century, various *professors* amused the crowd by diving off the pier in all manner of feats. These included Captain Camp, the one-legged swimmer, and Professor Reddish with his Bicycle Dive. In May 1912 Professor Cyril was performing his own version of the bicycle dive when he slipped, landed on the deck, fractured his skull and died.

From the 1900s to the 1960s, the West Pier became more and more a 'fun' pier with all the usual attractions. Close to the West Pier you can see the Brighton and Hove Pétanque Club in action.

CHRIS'S VERDICT: from almost total destruction to vibrant new life – we hope!
WALK TIME: n/a

Status: Grade I
Work started: April 1863
First opened: 5 October 1866
Designer: Eugenius Birch
Contractor: Laidlaw & Son, Glasgow
Construction: cast iron and wrought iron columns on screw piles, wrought iron bracing
Original length: 1115 ft (340 m)
Present length: n/a
Storm damage: 1896, 1987, 1988, 2002, 2003, 2004
Restoration: 1893, 1901, 1916, 1932, 1996
Legal: Brighton West Pier Acts & Orders 1866–1954
Original owners: Brighton West Pier Co.
Present owners: Brighton West Pier Trust
Support group: Friends of the West Pier
Website: www.westpier.co.uk

BURNHAM-ON-SEA

Burnham Pier beach, 1952 (courtesy of the National Piers Society)

OUR SHORTEST PIER, OR IS IT?

The great Victorian engineer Isambard Kingdom Brunel was the inspiration for this early twentieth-century pier pavilion which is similar in style to two of Brunel's magnificent railway stations, Bristol Temple Meads and Bath Spa. Brunel designed the old St Andrew's School which stood opposite the pier. True to the spirit of Brunel, Burnham Pier was the first to be constructed in reinforced concrete. Contrary to Brunel's style – build bigger and better! – Burnham Pier is claimed to be the shortest in Britain. Another claim for Burnham's pier is that it was the first to be illuminated. Reinforced concrete piles were used because of the strong tides in Bridgewater Bay. The concrete was made using granite chippings from Penryn in Cornwall and which are still used in maintaining the pier today. Engineers from all over Britain came to see it.

Plans to build a railway/steamer pier further down the promenade at Burnham in 1906 were never implemented. So, does the Burnham pavilion count as a pier? Supporters of Cleethorpes (335 feet) claim their pier is the shortest, and that Burnham's is merely a beach pavilion and that the Weymouth Bandstand Pier is, likewise, just a building on stilts. But, Burnham Pier does have a very fine pavilion, and its amusement arcade provides bingo, games, rides and has a café. You can sit under cover on the pier forecourt, where there is a designated smoking area. One of the two side walkways is open. There are no amusements on the promenade, but the town centre is close by. There is ample parking on the Esplanade by the pier.

Two piers were built at Burnham-on-Sea in rapid succession. The first, completed in 1910, was not strong enough to stand up to the strong currents and ebb tides at this point on the coast and soon disappeared. The existing pier/pavilion was built 1911–14 but was never extended. This pre-World War I pavilion is still providing shore-end entertainment, but with such a short pier, it could hardly be anywhere else!

After the terrible storm on Sunday, 13 December 1981, a new sea wall had to be built. It was proposed to demolish the pier, but a public outcry and personal interventions from then prime-minister Margaret Thatcher and MP David Heathcote-Amery saved the day. The Parkin family, members of the Showman's Guild of Great Britain, have run the pavilion as a family amusement centre since 1968. They bought the pier from Sedgemoor District Council in October 1995.

Currently in charge of the pier is Louise Parkin who was Mayor of Burnham-on-Sea in 2004/5. Seven generations of the Parkin family have been showmen. Her grandfather Bob Parkin ran a fairground boxing booth, the only one ever licensed by the British Board of Boxing Control. Louise is scathing about the claims of Weymouth Pier Bandstand to be shorter than Burnham: 'They chopped off the end of their pier, so that doesn't count,' she says, 'Burnham Pier is just as it was built.' Remarkably, Burnham Pier won a Britain in Bloom award seven years running.

Burnham Pier pavilion brightens a gloomy day (author's collection)

CHRIS'S VERDICT: the 'Brunel' pavilion is worth seeing
WALK TIME: 22 sec

Work started: (i) 1908; (ii) 1911
First opened: (i) 1910; (ii) 1914
Construction: reinforced concrete and steel
Original length: 117 ft (37 m)
Present length: 117 ft (37 m)
Storm damage: 1981
Restoration: 1990s
Legal: Burnham, Somerset, Pier Order 1906 & Act 1907
Original owners: Burnham Tidal Harbour & Railway Co.
Present owners: Parkin family
Website: www.burnham-on-sea.com

CLACTON

Clacton Pier entrance promises much inside (author's collection)

FUN FOR ALL

The approach to Clacton Pier is both dramatic and enticing. You walk down a slope and under an arched footbridge that Isambard Kingdon Brunel would have been proud of. The shallow arch, faced in stone and topped with a classic balustrade is a gem and looks perfect in its setting. Facing you is the pier entrance, colourful and inviting, but with only a hint of its many shore-end amusements.

Clacton Pier ('for Family Fun') has surely the best postal address of any pier: No. 1 North Sea. Clacton claims the distinction of being second only to Southsea Clarence in having the widest 'shore end' in the UK. The six and a half acre site includes a sea aquarium, Oscar's nightclub, a flight simulator and a big wheel. However, it also boasts the claim to 'the largest undercover fairground in East Anglia'.

The former theatre at the sea end of the pier has seen better days. Clad in corrugated sheeting somewhat resembling a 'tin tabernacle', much of it is now used for storage and only a small part of what was clearly a significant building is in public use as a café. Deckchairs are no longer for hire on the large boardwalk area on the hexagonal pier head, and one can understand why, but there is a distinct lack of fixed seating. Seats and shelters here would make an ideal area for sunbathing and viewing. Just beyond the boardwalk is the fishing jetty extension.

Clacton was a plain pier, 480 feet by 12 feet wide. The official opening was on 27 July 1871, just ahead of the first Bank Holiday on 7 August. Mainly a steamer landing stage for goods and passengers, Clacton Pier quickly became a popular venue for promenading. Admission was two pence. Pier-builder Peter Bruff installed a rail line along the length of the pier. Landing charges included 6*d.* for a barrel of gunpowder, 1*d.* per cubic foot for musical instruments, and £1 for a corpse.

A lifeboat station was added in 1878. On 4 July 1882, Bruff's railway to Clacton opened. It reduced the travel time from London to ninety minutes, as opposed to five hours by steamer. Once the railway had arrived, Clacton became a popular destination for Londoners, especially on day trips. It was decided to extend the pier and provide more facilities for visitors. In 1890–93 the pier was widened and extended to a design by Kinipple and Jaffrey. A new landing stage, a polygonal pier head and pavilion were built in 1893, making the pier 1,180 feet long. Due to operating difficulties, the Clacton Pier Co. was wound up in December 1897. The pier, valued at £51,112, was taken over by the newly-formed Coast Development Company which also owned seven Belle paddle steamers.

In 1922 Ernest Kingsman became the new owner of Clacton Pier. He built the Blue Lagoon Dance Hall (1922), the Lifeboat House (1928) and the shore-end Ocean Theatre (1928). The Crystal Casino and swimming pool were added in 1931/2 when the pier itself was widened. In 1940 Clacton pier was sectioned due to World War II, and the Crystal Casino and the children's theatre were demolished.

Clacton Pier, c.1957 (Frances Foote collection)

Clacton Pier, 1903 (courtesy of the National Piers Society)

Railway engineer Peter Schuyler Bruff (1812–1900) designed and built Clacton Pier despite a great deal of opposition. Bruff, known as the Brunel of the Eastern Counties, was engineer and manager of Eastern Union Railway. He recognised the potential of this little fishing village as a seaside holiday resort if easy access could be provided from London by rail and sea. The first building in the new town of Clacton-on-Sea, the 640-foot-long wooden pier was opened on 27 July 1871. The pier was financed by the London-based Woolwich Steam Packet Co. which in return had exclusive rights for their paddle steamers to land at the pier.

During World War II the pier was damaged by a floating mine. After the war the New Walton Pier Co. took over the pier, which later suffered further damage due to storms in 1978, 1979 and 1987. On 11 January 1978 there were exceptional high tides and strong winds along the east coast and the pier suffered £100,000-worth of damage. Just as repairs from the storm were being completed the following year, the pier again took a battering from the sea. There was damage to the Lifeboat House and the Dolphinarium, the latter requiring the hasty removal of a killer whale, a dolphin, sea lions and some penguins. The great 'hurricane' of 1987 also caused a lot of damage.

In 1981 Anglo-Austrian Automatics bought Clacton Pier for £2 million, but went into receivership in 1994. E & M Harrison Ltd. took over in October 1994 and immediately started renovation work. Clacton Pier now features a wide variety of family entertainments on its six-and-a-half acre site. Admission to the pier is free and many of the attractions are under cover, including the traditional rides like the waltzer and the dodgems. Among the pier's popular attractions are the Seaquarium and the Haunted Mansion.

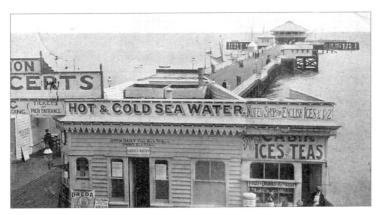

Clacton Pier, c.1909 (Frances Foote collection)

'Clacton Pier is not for the traditionalist, but it does unashamedly provide the brash, colourful entertainment loved by so many, that is now a feature of the popular British seaside resort' (The Heritage Trail) – just about sums it up. In keeping with its origins, Clacton Pier was host to MV *Balmoral* in 2007.

Stanley Holloway performed in concert parties at Clacton, and the comic and actor, Roy Hudd had two seasons at the Ocean Theatre. He tells the story: 'Most of the stagehands were lifeboatmen. When they got a call-out, they would quickly disappear, as did most of the audience who found the events outside more compelling than those inside!'

CHRIS'S VERDICT: lots to offer, but could do more
WALK TIME: 3 min 28 sec

Work started: 1870
First opened: 18 July 1871 (official opening: 27 July 1871)
Designer: Peter Schuyler Bruff
Construction: steel piles, pitch pine deck
Original length: (i) 480 ft (146 m); (ii) 1180 ft (360 m), 1893
Present length: 1,180 ft (360 m)
Storm damage: 1978, 1979, 1987
Restoration: 1890/3, 1922, 1931/2, 1994
Legal: Clacton on Sea Pier Act 1865
Original owners: Clacton Pier Co.
Present owners: E & M Harrison Ltd.
Website: www.clactonpier.org

CLEETHORPES

Cleethorpes – small pier, big beach (author's collection)

'THE TIMELESS PIER'

At 335 feet long, Cleethorpes is definitely a contender for the world's shortest pier. If you discount the pier pavilions at Burnham and Weymouth, this is definitely Britain's shortest seaside pleasure pier. But, remember, even the shortest piers have their own individual character and every pier has something to offer in the way of entertainment and recreation. An inviting entrance and a broad ramp under illuminated arches lead up to a handsome offset pavilion that rejoices in the name 'Pier 39' after the old steamer pier in San Francisco.

The pier pavilion saw service as a pub in the 1980s, and is now the Pier 39 nightclub. Looking to accommodate families as well as the 'groovy guys and chicks', the front area has been opened up for daytime use by visitors. This new facility was opened in 2006 by National Piers Society stalwart, Tim Mickleburgh, who lives in nearby Grimsby. Pier 39 also puts on events for the under-18s. Live bands regularly attract an audience of 1,200 on a Bank Holiday. The rock band Blur performed there in September 1995, and more recently the pier has hosted chart bands such as the Holloways and the Hoosiers.

There's only room for this one 'attraction' on the pier itself, but all the usual facilities are nearby at the adjoining promenade, including a road train and a first aid station that takes in 'lost' children. There is parking along the prom and close to the pier, but before you can collect your parking ticket you must first punch in the numbers – not the letters – of your car registration. If you arrive by train, Cleethorpes railway station is also just along the prom.

Twenty feet wide and 1,200 feet long, Cleethorpes Pier was built by the Head Wrightson company of Stockton for £8,000. It opened on August Bank Holiday Monday, 1873. Although an order had been placed in 1867, it was 1872 before work started. On the opening day, 2,859 visitors

Crowds on Cleethorpes Pier, c.1907
(Frances Foote collection)

Fire on Cleethorpes Pier, 1903
(courtesy of the National Piers Society)

paid 6*d*. each to go on the pier. Thirty-seven thousand people paid 1*d*. admission in the first five weeks. By 1909 admission had risen to 2*d*.

In 1884 the pier was leased to the Manchester, Sheffield & Lincolnshire Railway (later LNER) at £450 a year. Twenty years later the railway company bought the pier for £11,250. The sale price in 1981 was £55,000.

A concert hall was built on the pier head in 1888, but burned down in 1903. Two years later a new pavilion was put up at the shore end and a café and shops were built on the site of the original building. Originally, the new pavilion had no heating and was only used in summer, when there were concerts and popular dances throughout the week. The pavilion was also home to the Cleethorpes Musical Festival. Heating was finally installed in 1923 to allow year-round entertainment. The 1905 pavilion is still with us today, but the rest of the pier has gone.

Cleethorpes Council bought the pier from the LNER in 1936. A section of the pier was blown up in 1940, and after World War II, only the pavilion was re-opened to the public. The isolated seaward end was demolished. Interestingly, some of the salvaged material was utilised in constructing a new stand at Leicester City FC's Filbert Street soccer stadium. This reduced the length of the pier to 335 feet compared to its original length of 1,200 feet.

In 1968 the pavilion was modernised at a cost of £50,000. Facilities included a 600-seat concert hall that featured bingo and wrestling, presumably not at the same time! The big east coast storm and high tide on 11 January 1978 left more that 150 elderly and disabled people stranded on the pier. All were brought to safety.

Funworld Ltd. bought the pier from the council for £50,000 in 1981, but after a poor first season Funworld closed the pier in 1983 and demolition looked likely.

Two years later local businessman, Mark Mayer, bought the pier and spent £300,000 transforming the 1905 pavilion into a modern nightclub. The pier was re-opened on 4 September 1985. Whitegate Leisure plc took over in 1989 and spent £500,000 redeveloping the pavilion which reopened in April 1992. In that same year Whitegate Leisure increased its capacity from 560 to 800. Next year a shelter was added at a cost of £20,000. In 2007, new owner, Mr Kash Pungi, planned a £500,000 project to renew the pier legs with 40 tonnes of steel.

CHRIS'S VERDICT: small but perfectly formed
WALK TIME: 60 sec

Work started: 1872
First opened: 1873
Designer: Cleethorpes J E & A Dowson
Contractor: Head Wrightson, Stockton-on-Tees
Construction: raked tubular iron piles, arched iron cross-beams, timber deck
Original length: 1200 ft (366 m)
Present length: 335 ft (102 m)
Fire: 1903
Restoration: 1888, 1905, 1968, 1983–5, 1989–93
Legal: Clacton New Pier Order 1867 and Act 1873
Original owners: Cleethorpes Promenade & Pier Co.
Present owners: H Kash Pungi
Websites: www.cleethorpes-online.co.uk, www.welovehtepier.com

CLEVEDON

Recent view of Clevedon Pier (courtesy of Linda Strong)

POSSIBLY BRITAIN'S BEST-LOOKING PIER

'As delicate as a Japanese print in the mist, and like an insect in the sunlight'
– Sir John Betjeman

Seeing Clevedon Pier for the first time, you cannot fail to be impressed by the beauty of its delicate arched spans. Completely uncluttered, and with a castle-like entrance building at the shore end, a Japanese-style pavilion, two small Victorian shelters at the head, plus its dramatic location, this is a pier to be admired from every angle even before you have set foot through the fine wrought iron gates at the pier entrance.

Then there's the sheer joy of going out to sea just for the pleasure of it. There is wooden seating all along both sides of the pier neck. The sea-end pavilion, which has a small café operating in the summer months, provides a superb first-storey viewing platform. The panoramic views take in the new Severn crossing, the pier's one telescope being strategically placed at the pier end.

Apart from the tollhouse shop – which has a first-floor art gallery – and the café, the pier has no other commercial operations and relies on tolls, donations and fund-raising for its upkeep. At £1.50 for adults, £1 for OAPs and 75p for children, toll charges are, necessarily, relatively high. Unlike the Victorians, who charged extra for bath-chairs and invalid carriages, wheelchairs go free. As well as paying the toll, you can support the pier by playing its lottery or by leaving a legacy in your will.

Clevedon Pier is perhaps the best enduring British pier still much in its original form. This Grade I listed structure is noted for its 180 feet of masonry at the shore end and its lacy, 'spider's web' ironwork of eight 100 feet-tall arched spans. The pier legs are made up wrought iron Barlow

Rails, riveted back-to back to make a component stronger than the usual circular hollow piles. Barlow Rails were taken from the Great Western Railway when it was reduced in width from Brunel's broad gauge to the narrower standard gauge. Lengthwise, there are two three-feet-6-inch-deep composite girders. Construction of the pier was particularly difficult due to the 47-foot tidal range – the second-highest in the world – and the five-knot current. Because of the tidal range, Clevedon Pier was built unusually high at 68 feet. Built in 1869 from factory-made components and assembled on site, there were 370 tons of wrought iron in the pier frame, and 5.6 miles of planking on its 16.5-feet-wide deck. On Easter Monday, 29 March 1869, there was a gala opening, when the 10.15 a.m. train from Bristol alone brought 500 passengers for the occasion.

Lady Margaret Ann Elton recalled: 'There was a general holiday and floral arches had sprouted up all over the town. Altogether, two thousand people came by the Bristol and Exeter line, along with hundreds of carts poured in from the country. Finally assembled, a great procession left the terminus, consisting of twelve policemen, fifty-four members of the Clevedon Artillery and Band, ninety-four Nailsea Engineers and their Band, the directors of the Clevedon and Weston Pier Companies, twenty-eight members of the Committee of Demonstration, inhabitants and visitors, the Bristol Artillery Band, ninety Odd Fellows, the Axbridge Drum and Fife Boys, and five hundred school children.'

A huge triumphal arch across the Marine Parade carried the inscription: 'Success to the Pier'. At 1.30 p.m. the 500 children sang Psalm 148. There was a short service of dedication, in which the local clergy hinted that the opening of the pier should not be allowed to interfere with the observance of the Sabbath. Then there was a cannon volley fired by the First Somerset Artillery, the massed bands played the National Anthem, and Clevedon Pier was open for the good of the townspeople and the benefits which they believed the pier would bring.

Weston-super-Mare architect, Hans Price, designed the ornate castellated pier tollhouse, turnstiles, gates and railings. He was also responsible for redesigning the adjacent Rock House and the Royal Pier Hotel. This work, which included alterations to prevent people using the pier from seeing hotel guests going to and from the privies, was completed in 1869. In 1886 the original *Waverley* paddle steamer made its first call. By 1897 the charge between Clevedon and Weston-super-Mare was 1*s*. 6*d*. return.

In 1891 the pier was in difficulties, due to its high operating costs. When it was decided to sell the pier for £700, Sir Edmund Elton, the biggest shareholder, bought up all the other shares and donated the pier to the local council. Next year the original wooden landing stage was replaced by a larger cast-iron one, angled to be in line with the tidal flows. More buildings were added and the pier head was enlarged. Sir Edmund opened the new pier head and landing stage on 3 April 1893. The Japanese pavilion and shelters were built the following year.

In January 1899 a storm ripped out 20 feet of the pier deck. In 1910 the landing stage was wrecked in a gale, and it was 30 April 1913 before a new concrete stage came into operation. It had cost £300. From 1952 the council had the pier tested regularly for safety, and on 16 October 1970, two spans collapsed while being tested. There was a campaign to save it and the pier was given Grade II* listed building status. In July 1979 Woodspring District Council applied for permission to demolish the pier, but following a public inquiry in March of the following year, this was withdrawn. In the words of the then Environment Secretary, Michael Heseltine MP, Clevedon Pier was 'an exceptionally important building, warranting every effort to preserve it'.

For nearly twenty years Clevdon Pier remained closed. Under the Clevedon Pier Preservation Trust, restoration work finally began in May 1982. The following year the Trust was awarded £2.5 million in grants from the Heritage Memorial Fund and the Historic Buildings and Monuments Commission. In 1985 the pier neck was dismantled, taken to Portishead, restored and re-erected in 1988. The pier re-opened on 27 May 1989. A further Lottery grant in 1995 allowed the full restoration of the pier head and landing stage. On 29 May 1998, the pier was re-opened by Sir Charles Elton Bart, great-great-grandson of the Chairman of the original pier company. The total cost of £3.2 million had been raised with the help of local fund-raising and grants from the District and Town Councils and the National Lottery.

Ready for your walk (author's collection)

Clevedon Pier, c.1906, much as it is now
(Frances Foote collection)

Sunset on Clevedon Pier (courtesy of Linda Strong)

Clevedon Pier got a Civic Trust award in 1999, the year it was made Pier of the Year. It came second in the 2007 awards. In January 2001 Clevedon Pier's listing was upgraded from Grade II* to Grade I. By 2007 the number of plaques donated for the pier's upkeep was approaching 10,000. Clevedon's fund-raising event, 'Walk the Plank', on 22 April 2007, saw a new record set for the longest distance walked on the pier in a day, 80 laps (a lap being out and back), amounting to 26.6 miles.

CHRIS'S VERDICT: slim, delicate and beautiful
WALK TIME: 2 min 56 sec

Status: Grade I
Work started: 1867
First opened: 29 March 1869
Designer: Richard J Ward, John William Grover (their only pier)
Contractor: Hamilton Windsor
Construction: wrought iron girders on wrought iron columns and screw piles
Original length: 842 ft (257 m)
Present length: 842 ft (257 m)
Storm damage: 1891, 1910
Fire: 1903
Restoration: 1888, 1905, 1968, 1983–85, 1989–92
Legal: Clevedon Pier Acts and Orders 1864–88
Original owners: Clevedon Pier Co.
Present owners: Clevedon Pier & Heritage Trust Ltd.
Pier of the Year: 1999
E-mail: enquiries@clevedonpier.com
Website: www.clevedonpier.com

COLWYN BAY VICTORIA

Victoria Pier, c.1910 (Frances Foote collection)

LIVING ON THE PIER

If you sold your house to buy a pier, where would you live? On the pier of course. That's exactly what Steve Hunt did in December 2003 when, at 31, he became the youngest ever pier owner. 'It was a bit of a childhood fascination ever since I went to the coast as a young boy with my parents. I have always been fascinated by them, always wanted one. This one came up for sale so I bought it. I suppose anyone who buys an enormous 104-year-old iron structure standing in salt water probably ought to have their marbles checked,' he told BBC Wales.

Colwyn Bay Victoria Pier has had more than its fair share of disasters. Made from prefabricated parts, with decorative capitals supporting horizontal lattice girders, it was 220 feet long and 40 feet wide, and carried a 2,500-seat Moorish-style pavilion. The pier was opened on 1 June 1900 and was illuminated at night. In 1904 the pier was extended to its present length of 750 feet. A 600-seat Bijou Theatre was built on the pier head in 1916 and, along with the main pavilion, used to entertain troops stationed in Colwyn Bay during World War I. The pavilion burned down in 1922 and in 1923 was replaced by the local council, the pier's new owners, with a £45,000 art deco pavilion. This in turn burned down in 1933. A third, 'modern' pavilion which still stands, was put up in 1934. The Bijou had also burned down with the pavilion in 1933 but was never replaced.

The third and final pavilion incorporated murals by the famous war artist Eric Ravilious (1903–1942). It had a sprung maple floor for dancing and seated 700–750 patrons. 'There is a stimulating gaiety about the exterior and interior' said the magazine *Architect & Building News*. In 1958 the ballroom was closed, but worse was to follow. In 1968 the council sold the pier to the Trust House Forte (THF) who converted the pavilion into an American-style Dixieland Showbar. The ornate entrance gates and tollbooths were demolished to make way for the Golden Goose amusement arcade.

Mid-pier pavilion is closed (author's collection)

In 1976 THF applied to demolish the seaward end of the pier, but permission was refused by Colwyn Borough Council following a 4,000-signature petition. Parker Leisure Holdings bought the pier in 1979 and turned the showbar into a disco. With an estimated repair bill of £250,000, Parker Leisure in turn applied to demolish the pier in 1987. This was again refused, and in 1991 the pier was closed and put up for sale with £850,000 quoted as the cost of a complete refurbishment. In 1994 Mike and Ann Paxman bought the pier and reopened it the following year. Facilities included a café, shops and the Victoria Bar. The Paxmans lived on the pier, but were unable to achieve their aim of turning it into a major tourist attraction. Now Steve Hunt has taken up the challenge after buying the pier for a six-figure sum. *The Circus of Horrors* in November 2004 was the pier's first live show for twenty years.

Mixture of styles at pier entrance (author's collection)

Approaching Colwyn Bay from the east, don't be taken in by the two piers you first see. They are industrial structures, supplying stone and aggregate to be transported by sea. But do turn off the A55 for 'Old Colwyn and Promenade' to get directly to the Victoria pier and have a good view of it as you approach. There is ample car parking close by. The main pavilion is offset to the right, near the shore end. The vertical piles have minimal cross-bracing, and the deck is supported on wooden beams. The fancy ironwork balustrading is well-maintained, but the 'art deco' pavilion looks a mess.

Morecambe and Wise, Ken Dodd and Harry Secombe have all appeared at the pier theatre. It also saw the debut performance of boy soprano David Ivor Davies, better known as Ivor Novello.

Sad to say, the mid-pier pavilion is in a very bad way. While some of the original cast iron balustrading has been repainted, much remains to be done. Most of the pier deck is closed off to the public, other than to anglers, awaiting much-needed repairs, but you can sit out on the deck behind the shore-end pavilion and enjoy the sea air and the views along the coast to the west.

Owner Steve Hunt is doing his best to attract more people to the pier. In 2007, having completed his 'all new pier café', he was about to revamp the bar with windows to open up the eastern aspect. The problem he has in applying for Lottery and other grant funding is that the pier is privately-owned.

Name those cars in front of the pier! Victoria Pier, c.1958 (Frances Foote collection)

CHRIS'S VERDICT: a fine old pier in need of lots of cash
WALK TIME: 2 min 11 sec (part only)

Status: Grade II
Work started: June 1899
First opened: 1 June 1900
Designer: Maynall & Littlewood, Manchester
Contractor: Widnes Foundry Co.
Construction: braced cast iron columns, steel girders, timber deck members
Original length: (i) 220 ft (67 m); (ii) 750 ft (229 m), 1903
Present length: 750 ft (229 m)
Fire: 1922, 1933, 1935
Restoration: 1903, 1917, 1954, 1964–9, 2004– present
Original owners: Victoria Pier Co.
Present owner: Steve Hunt
Support group: Friends of the Pier
Website: www.victoriapier.com

CROMER

Superbly sinuous entrance steps (author's collection)

'AN ESPLANADY SORT OF PLACE'
– A C Swinburne 1880

Cromer Pier has a magnificent front – and the rest of it is pretty special too. You approach this most classic of piers up a wonderfully sinuous flight of stone steps, the like of which I have never seen anywhere else. In front of you is the truly outstanding, almost awe-inspiring colonnaded entrance, flanked by two supporting, circular buildings with cupolas that look exactly right in shape, scale and colour.

But as you ascend this gently rising staircase, your attention is drawn downwards. Set in stone – and rightly so – are the glorious feats of the local lifeboat crews and their coxwains in saving so many lives over the years. I counted a total of 247 people rescued from 1867 to 1998, but I could be wrong. The Cromer lifeboat station is at the end of the pier. Work was under way to update the slipway and boathouse to accommodate the new £2.5 million Tamar class lifeboat *Lester*, currently 'in build' at DML in Plymouth.

There are none of the usual 'amusements' on Cromer Pier or in its immediate vicinity. These are discretely situated a little way along the promenade. But – fear not! – there is the Pavilion Theatre, quite grand, and you can get a drink and an ice cream too on the pier. But you get the impression that any untoward jollity would be frowned upon, quite severely. The pier offers a gift shop and the Tides Restaurant, again quite restrained. Even the necessary wheelie bins are painted white, off-white of course, so they do not offend the eye. You get marvellous views of Cromer Pier from the Hotel de Paris and other more modest establishments on the cliff top.

Cromer, famous for its crabs, has one of the first seaside pleasure piers to be built in the twentieth century. But the town has records of a pier or jetty going back hundreds of years. Letters patent dated in the year 1390 refer to the 'pere' at 'crownmere'. In 1589 the pier reeves were reminded of their obligation to keep the pier in good order. A note of the pier being repaired is dated 1664, and a 1731 deed reads 'an undertaking was then on foot for making and erection of a pier'. In March 1820 the 'jettee' was washed away. Another was built and opened on 17 April 1821. This 210-foot wooden jetty was damaged by a gale on 18 February 1836 and in 1843 it was washed away

A new, 240-foot jetty, became the fashionable venue for an evening stroll. Couples were strictly supervised by the pier keeper who made sure that 'no improper person' frequented the pier, and that 'good order' was maintained at all times. The present Cromer Pier has much of the character of its predecessor. 'Promenading' is still popular, although there is no official to ensure correct behaviour. There are summer shows and Sunday concerts in the pavilion, and fishing from the pier head. There are no amusement machines on Cromer Pier and admission is free, but anglers must pay the required fees.

During an exceptionally high tide in 1897 a ship carrying coal – most likely from Newcastle to London – collided with the jetty and did so much damage repair proved to be an uneconomical option. The remaining structure was dismantled and the timber sold off for £40.

The 1899 Cromer Protection Act gave the Cromer Protection Commissioners authority to build a new pier. Work began on the 450-foot (136 m) pier in 1900 at a cost of £17,067 14s. 5d. Lord Claude Hamilton opened the pier on 8 June the following year. It had a short, wide deck, glass-screened shelters, and a bandstand at the sea end. In 1905 this was extended to form a pavilion. Three years later a maple-wood floor was installed for roller-skating. On 10 September 1846 the bylaws by the Protection Commissioners ruled that smoking on the pier was banned until after 9 p.m., by which time it was assumed that the ladies had left the pier. What the women did after 9 p.m. was of little concern, apparently. The Commission voted against having women's conveniences on the pier in 1908 and again in 1914. But on 26 June 1925 the decision was finally made to provide conveniences for both men and women on the pier. For this relief, much thanks. A lifeboat station was added in 1923.

In 1930 57 of the 91 piles were encased in concrete. A section of decking was removed in 1940, so planks had to be used to bridge the gap and reach the sea-end lifeboat station when there was a

Cromer Pier Bandstand, 1901
(courtesy of Poppyland Publishing)

Cromer Pier, c.1904
(courtesy of the National Piers Society)

Morris dancing on Cromer Pier, 2003
(courtesy of Poppyland Publishing)

call-out. The two halves of the pier were re-connected permanently in 1949. The 1953 gales caused a great deal of damage, but the pier was strengthened that year and again in 1968. On Britain's exposed east coast, Cromer Pier also suffered storm damage in 1949, 1976 and 1978. A gale ripped out the Amusement Arcade in February 1990 and it was not replaced.

On Sunday, 14 November 1993 the 80-ton working platform *Tayjack 1* broke its moorings, hit the pier and cut it in two. Thirty-six metres of deck was destroyed. A temporary bridge was put up to link the pier with the theatre and lifeboat station. Repairs were made in time for the 1994 season. The reconstruction work by contractors Dossor East earned them the first National Piers Society Peter Mason Award for engineering excellence in 1997. The old lifeboat house and launching ramp were temporarily removed in 1997 in preparation for a replacement station.

In 1985 Cromer Pier became part of the North Sea oil and gas industry when it was fitted with a new tide gauge by Shell Expro to help with their offshore surveys and for official tide study.

The pier pavilion was re-opened by actor Stephen Fry on 27 June 2004, but was damaged by a storm early the following year. In 2006 North Norfolk District Council valued Cromer Pier at just £1 (yes, one pound), but the council has had it insured for £4.3 million – the cost of total replacement.

Artists who have performed at Cromer Pier include: George Robey (1921), Robb Wilton (1937), Wee Georgie Wood, Vic Oliver (1938), Chris Barber and his Band (1957), Semprini, Bryan Johnson (1960), ventriloquist Peter Brough and his puppet Archie Andrews, baritone Owen Brannigan (1961), DJ David Jacobs (1964), pianist Walter Landauer, actor–entertainer Bill Pertwee (1973), Humphrey Lyttleton and his Band (1978), folk singer Richard Digance, jazz singer George Melly, comedian Sandy Powell, Syd Lawrence and his orchestra (1979), jazzman Acker Bilk, singer Frank Ifield, Vilem Tausky and the Palm Court Orchestra, the National Youth Orchestra (1980), The Temperance Seven (1963), violinist Max Jaffa (1987), singer Val Doonican (1989), former Ultravox frontman Midge Ure (1995), singer–comedian Max Bygraves, 'comic in a frock' Danny La Rue, ventriloquist Ray Allen and his Lord Charles (1997). Other names are Dennis Lotis, Rosemary Squires, Joe Brown, magician Paul Daniels, and folk rock band Fairport Convention.

Cromer Pier has since earned a national reputation for being the last to show genuine 'end of the pier' shows with no big stars. But when the National Piers Society had their AGM at Cromer in 2000, actor Hugh Grant was seen in the bar after the show.

CHRIS'S VERDICT: definitely one for the purist – a wonderful pier, a feast for the eye
WALK TIME: 1 min 48 sec

Status: Grade II
Work started: 1900
First opened: 8 June 1901
Designer: Douglass & Arnott (their only pier)
Contractor: Alfred Thorne
Construction: steelwork
Original length: 500 ft (153 m)
Present length: 500 ft (153 m)
Storm damage: 1949, 1953, 1976, 1978, 1990
Ship collisions: 1993
Restoration: 1905, 1908, 1930, 1955, 1968, 1993
Legal: Cromer Protection Act 1899, Cromer UDC Act 1948
Original owners: Cromer Protection Commissioners
Present owners: North Norfolk District Council
Pier of the Year: 2000

DEAL

Put out more flags – it's a new Deal (author's collection)

CONCRETE CAN LOOK GOOD

Deal Pier was the UK's first new post-war pier, but there were two other piers here previously. The stylish concrete pier we see today was built in the 1950s to replace its Victorian predecessor which had been demolished in World War II to help the war effort. The first pier was started in 1838 to a design by J Rennie. It was planned to be 445 feet long with a budget of £21,000, but the pier company ran out of money after spending £12,000, and only 250 feet of the pier was completed. This was enough to attract some steamer trade. After being damaged by sandworms, in 1857, a storm destroyed the whole structure which was washed up on the beach. The remains were sold for scrap for a paltry £50.

A new 1,100-foot iron pier was built by Laidlaw to a Birch design. Work started in the spring of 1863, and the new pier opened on 8 November 1864. There were two ornate tollhouses and a baggage tramway along the length of the pier. It was officially opened in the autumn of 1864 by local MP Mr Knatchbull-Hugessen. A reading room and salt baths were added in the 1870s. On 19 January 1873 the barque *Merle* hit the pier during a storm and caused extensive damage. On 26 January 1884 the schooner *Alliance* also ran into the pier during a storm. Repairs were made and a pier-head pavilion was built in 1886. In 1920 Deal Council bought the pier for £10,000.

The pier was 'sectioned' in 1940 and was twice hit by ships in World War II. On Sunday, 29 January 1940 the 350-ton Dutch vessel, *Nora,* anchored a mile off Deal, was hit by a drifting magnetic mine which blew a hole in the ship's side. After the crew were evacuated, the *Nora* was beached 50 yards south of Deal pier. Despite warnings from local fishermen, the ship was not secured and the rising tide continually smashed the ship against the pier and eventually right through it, taking 200 feet of ironwork onto her decks. The pier was not repaired and was finally removed by the Army.

Winston Churchill, then Lord of the Admiralty and soon to become our wartime prime minister, surveyed the scene. He gave permission for the Army to demolish the pier to give the coastal guns a clear line of sight. Only the tollhouses remained and they were removed in 1954 when work on the new pier began.

Deal's third pier, built by Sir William Halcrow and Partners at a cost of £750,000, was opened by the Duke of Edinburgh on 19 November 1957. It is 1,026 feet (313 metres) long, only slightly shorter than Birch's Victorian classic. After half a century of exposure to the elements, the concrete arches still look as good as new, a tribute to the pier's design and construction. The pier head has a three-stage landing and fishing platform. The pier head café was due to be demolished in 2007 and rebuilt for the 2008 season. Deal Pier's front approach is welcoming, set off by a fine statue that everyone can appreciate. Created by artist Jon Buck in 1998 and entitled 'Embracing the Sea', it shows a well-muscled bloke wrestling with four fish. Now that's my kind of art! In 2006 a teenage angler landed an 11 lb lobster that experts believe could be more than 100 years old.

The pier is lit at night, and at weekends during high season there is twenty-four hour opening.

Deal Pier severed after Nora *collision, 29 January 1940 (Richard Riding collection)*

Deal Pier twisted after Nora *collision, 29 January 1940 (Richard Riding collection)*

Deal Esplanade and Pier, c.1910 (Frances Foote collection)

Rainbow over Deal Pier (Norman collection)

CHRIS'S VERDICT: well-kept, stylish and modern
WALK TIME: 3 min 01sec

Status: Grade II
Work started: (i) 1838; (ii) 1863; (iii) 1954
First opened: (i) 1838; (ii) 8 November 1864; (iii) 19 November 1957
Designer: (i) J Rennie (his only pier); (ii) Eugenius Birch; (iii) Sir W Halcrow & Partners
Contractor: (ii) Laidlaw; (iii) Sir W Halcrow & Ptnrs.
Construction: (i) timber; (ii) wrought and cast iron; (iii) hollow steel piles surrounded by concrete, steel beams encased in concrete, concrete decking
Original length: (i) 250 ft (76 m); (ii) 1100 ft (336 m);
Present length: 1026 ft (313 m)
Landing stage: yes
Storm damage: 1949, 1953, 1976, 1978, 1990
Ship collisions: 1873, 1884, 1940
Restoration: 1905, 1908, 1930, 1955, 1968. 1993
Original owners: (i) Deal Pier Co; (ii) Deal & Walmer Pier Co.
Legal: Deal Pier Order 1920
Present owners: Dover District Council
Website: www.dealpier.com

EASTBOURNE

Pier deck and sea end pavilion, 1904 (courtesy of the National Piers Society)

A GRAND PIER

Eastbourne Pier is anything but modest. Bold and brash, it announces itself as 'Britain's favourite Pier' and 'Europe's No. 1 Pier'. But when you see this attractive pier illuminated at night, you can see why it was voted Pier of the Year in 1996.

The pier carries a whole series of commanding buildings, starting with a turreted fish and chip emporium. Then there is the main pavilion with its huge domed roof, followed by several small pavilions and shelters. The handsome sea-end pavilion with its small 'onion dome' perched on top provides a definitive end stop. The predominant colour is silver, which shines and sparkles in the sun – magical!

This pier is unusual in that the deck slopes down midway. There are seats and deckchairs near the end of the pier. The fancy rails are simply made to lean on and gaze out to sea. There are great views on both sides, with Beachey Head to the west. The pier has plenty of facilities, including a café, family pub and a nightclub. The far-end pavilion houses the recently restored camera obscura. There is also fishing on the old landing stage. Eastbourne's lower promenade runs under the pier – always an advantage, I feel. It's a good viewing place for Eastbourne's annual 'Birdman' competition which began in 1995.

It took six years to build this pier. The first pile was driven on 18 April 1866. Lord Edward Cavendish officially opened the pier on 13 June 1870, but the job was not finally completed until 1872. Designed by Birch and built by J E Dowson and Head Wrightson, it cost £13,400 and included a landing stage, kiosk and windbreak. The piles rested on specially-made cups that sat on the rock bed beneath the sand. This allows the pier to 'give' under severe weather conditions.

The Duke of Devonshire owned most of the land. Covenants on various types of buildings ensured there was no music on a Sunday, not even by the Salvation Army. The pier was damaged by a storm on 1 January 1877 which destroyed the shoreward end of the pier. Birch replaced the damaged section at higher level. 'Mr. Wolfe's German Band' was engaged for the pier's first season. The twelve players each got £3 for playing four times a day, seven days a week. Later the band was given one day a week off. The German Band was followed by a 16-strong Hanovarian band which played from 1 June to 31 October for a £250 fee.

A domed 400-seat theatre was built at the pier head in 1888 for £250. This was replaced by a 1,000-seat theatre, camera obscura and pier office complex in 1889–1901 at a cost of £30,000, the original theatre finding a new role as a cattle shed. In 1893 a three-berth landing stage was added, and two mid-way saloons followed in 1901. In 1912 new entrance buildings were built, and, in 1925, a 900-seat music pavilion was erected at the shore end. This was used as a ballroom and later became an amusement arcade.

In 1940 the authorities considered blowing up the pier, but decking was removed instead. Machine guns were installed in the pier theatre. Due to the shortage of timber after the war, concrete decking was used as a replacement. The year 1951 saw the construction of a new kidney-shaped entrance building. Trust House Forte (THF) took over the pier in 1968. In January 1970 the theatre, where Norman Wisdom and Sandy Powell had played, burned down. It was rebuilt as the Dixieland Show Bar and was mainly used for discos and cabaret. In 1985 a new arcade was built as part of a £250,000 refurbishment.

Eastbourne Pier from the east (author's collection)

Eastbourne Pier deck, c.1937 (courtesy of Northern Writers)

In October 1987, the landing stage was wrecked by the 'hurricane' – the Great Storm of 1987 – but new owners First Leisure plc continued to develop the pier. This was the infamous 'not a hurricane' as described so memorably on BBC TV by weather forecaster Michael Fish. The Duke of Devonshire opened a new £500,000 entrance building on 15 June 1991. The refurbished camera obscura was opened to the public in 2003. The 'bootleg' birdman rally was cancelled 2005, but the round-the-pier raft race went ahead. MV *Balmoral* called at Eastbourne in 2007.

The 'New Pavilion', c.1928 (courtesy of the National Piers Society)

CHRIS'S VERDICT: a grand pier in every way
WALK TIME: 2 min 59 sec

Status: Grade II
Work started: 18 April 1866
First opened: 13 June 1870 (completed 1872)
Designer: Eugenius Birch
Contractors: J E Dowson & Head Wrightson
Construction: raked and vertical cast iron screw piles supporting lattice girders; iron and wood frame
Original length: 1000 ft (305 m)
Present length: 1000 ft (305 m)
Storm damage: 1877
Restoration: 1878, 1888, 1889–1901, 1912, 1925, 1951, 1971, 1985, 1990/01
Original owners: Eastbourne Pier Co.
Legal: Eastbourne Pier Orders 1864–1900
Present owners: Six Piers Ltd.
Pier of the Year: 1996
Website: www.eastbournepier.com

FALMOUTH PRINCE OF WALES

Prince of Wales Pier from the Marks & Sparks café (author's collection)

GEM IN A BEAUTIFUL SETTING

Falmouth Harbour on the south coast of Cornwall is about as picturesque as you can get, but it is a busy working port with a tremendous amount of activity and many ferry services from three different piers. The Prince of Wales Pier is part solid groin and part open construction with reinforced concrete piles. Primarily a well-used ferry terminal with five landing berths, the Prince of Wales Pier qualifies as a pleasure pier – in my humble opinion – as it offers plenty of space to sit, stroll and enjoy the harbour views. You can also sit out on the pier and take refreshment from the 'pier café with sun deck', as it is advertised. Not that I want to advertise, but if for any reason (weather … shopping) you are in the nearby Marks and Spencer, their café has great views over the pier and harbour.

The pier's stone section is very broad. There are seats and solid 1950s-type shelters on the extension, and a solid wooden rail all round on a concrete plinth. The deck is surfaced with asphalt. I was surprised to be told that the No. 1 berth has a half-hour service to Flushing, but this is Flushing-just-across-the-water (you could almost skip a stone from bank to bank) and not Flushing in Holland.

Duplicate plaques tell you that the foundation stone was laid by HRH the Prince of Wales (so that's where the name came from!) on 20 July 1903. He later became George V, the 'Sailor King'. William Banks was the Mayor and W H Tresidder the engineer. The Rt Hon John, Earl of Kimberley, opened the pier on 5 May 1905. Joseph Gross JP was now the mayor and E H Page was the contractor. During World War II the Americans took over the pier and built storage tanks underneath. The pier re-opened to the public in April 1951.

This is what *Engineering Timelines* had to say about the Prince of Wales (the pier that is): 'this reinforced concrete pier was built as an extension to the existing masonry wharf at Falmouth's thriving port and dockyards. It juts out at a right angle to the wharf, to a length of 900 ft[*] The Hennebique-concrete deck is 36 ft wide and 5 in thick. At every 20 ft 3 in interval stands a trestle of three reinforced concrete piles, supporting the deck and descending 30 ft to the seabed. These are "sleeved" in mass concrete – an early example of the technique – giving them the appearance of solid columns. Sleeving was used to provide greater stability because the piles are sunk only 8 ft into the ocean floor, where they meet rock.' So now you know.

[* not according to me! Ten spans of twenty feet or so is about 200 feet of open structure, plus about 300 feet of solid groin which equals 500 feet. I rest my case.]

Falmouth Harbour, including the Carrick Roads, is reputed to be the third largest natural harbour in the world. The first Harbour Master was appointed in 1870 at a salary of £150 a year. Men above 55 years and below the age of 32 were excluded from the post. Captain Richard Sherris was given the job on 19 September 1870. The first five men employed by the Commissioners all had the same Christian name: William Henry Worsdel, William Henry Rule, William John Barbery, William May, William Thomas Hall and William Andrew. They and Captain Sherris were all sworn in as special constables and in fact became the harbour police.

There have been two major post-war restorations of the pier, in 1951 and 1987. The latter cost £23,000. At one time, a scheme was mooted to fill in part of the harbour and incorporate the Prince of Wales Pier into a new harbour wall, but thankfully this idea came to nothing.

Prince of Wales Pier, c.1918 – hardly looks different today (Frances Foote collection)

CHRIS'S VERDICT: definitely a pleasure pier
WALK TIME: 1 min 12 sec

Work started: 20 July 1903
First opened: 5 May 1905
Designer: W H Tresidder
Contractor: E H Page
Construction: solid stone groin with extension of reinforced concrete piles
Original length: 510 ft (156 m)
Present length: 510 ft (156 m)
Restoration: 1951, 1987
Present owners: Carrick District Council
Websites: www.engineering-timelines.com, www.falmouthport.co.uk, (the Harbour Commissioners), www.
princeofwales-falmouth.co.uk (ok, so it's a pub)

FELIXSTOWE

Felixstowe Pier, c.1906 (courtesy of the National Piers Society)

TOO GOOD TO LOSE

Felixstowe Pier describes itself as 'The Pier', and why not? There is 'fun for all the family', but only at the land end. Go through the amusement arcade and you cannot progress beyond the kiddies' raceway. It just about qualifies for a timed walk, but only just. The pier deck looks in good condition, so hopefully it can and will be restored to full health. From the shore, it seems there is a row of shelters halfway along the pier neck and a small pavilion two thirds of the way along to its plain end – there is no sea-end 'T'.

Opposite the pier entrance is a leisure centre, and across the road a row of shops and cafes and a pub. Set in the Pier Bight car park forecourt is an unusual flat sundial of very recent vintage but all the more welcome for that. When telling the time by the sun, remember to stand on the block with the name of the current month on it. The points of the compass are shown, and you can impress your companions by 'boxing the compass'. Four points gets you 'nil point', eight is ok but sixteen gets the prize. Thirty-two points and you must have been a sea scout.

This is a pier with navigation lights at its head, due to the close proximity of the port of Felixstowe. Admission to the pier – or what remains of it – is free, with charges for fishing. When Felixstowe pier opened in August 1905 it was half a mile long. With the welfare of visitors and passengers in mind, there was a 42-inch gauge electric tramway along the deck. This was a state-of-the-art single-track electric railway with a central rail for the electric current. Tickets were one penny (old money). Later it was two pence for adults and one pence for children.

Felixstowe Pier was built to a simple design for the Coast Development Company (CDC) and marked the return to timber for pier construction. Imported timber like Jarrah and Greenheart is much more resistant to worm attack. The CDC was formed in 1898 when Belle Steamers Ltd.

teamed up with local businesses to build and promote piers in their mutual interest. With piers at Felixstowe, Southwold and Lowestoft, the CDC had a near monopoly on the local steamer trade on the East Anglian coast. But in 1905 the CDC was wound up and replaced by the Coast Development Corporation Ltd. That in turn went into liquidation in 1915 and was wound up in 1922. East Coast Piers, who had been keeping the tramway going, albeit only during the summer, took over the pier.

The tramway stopped operating at the start of World War II in 1939, and never resumed. After suffering the usual 'sectioning' inflicted on piers on the south and east coasts, the seaward end was demolished after the war. In 1995 a child overshot the slide and went into the sea, happily without serious consequences. But, by 1996, the pier was in danger of imminent collapse, and a £2.5 million rebuilding scheme was planned, however, it did not come to fruition. A charitable trust formed in 1999 to save the future of Felixstowe Pier eventually had to wind up, and the pier reverted to owners Pier Amusements Ltd. who applied for a demolition order in 2004.

Square and solid pavilion
(author's collection)

So far and no further – much of the deck is closed off
(author's collection)

Pier deck, c.1905 (courtesy of the National Piers Society)

CHRIS'S VERDICT: crying out to be re-opened
WALK TIME: n/a

Work started: 1903
First opened: August 1905
Contractor: Rogers Bros
Construction: timber, concrete decking
Original length: 2640 ft (805 m)
Present length: 450 ft (136 m)
Legal: Felixstowe Pier Order & Act 1900 and 1947
Original owners: Coast Development Co.
Present owners: Pier Amusements Ltd.
Websites: www.pier2pier.org, www.geograph.org.uk

FLEETWOOD VICTORIA

Still advertising its long-closed nightclub (author's collection)

New life for the last of the great British piers?

A sad sight – a derelict pier, apparently on its last legs. The pavilion looks safe enough, with its amusement arcade, pub and nightclub (all closed, mind) but the neck and pier head are in need of major renovation if they are to survive. And it is so ugly! The neck and platform above the superstructure are cast in concrete, and concrete, especially plain concrete, simply does not weather well. Any rescue mission must either remove or cover up this eyesore. The views across to Morecambe Bay are stunning, but will we ever be able once again to enjoy them from Fleetwood Pier?

But there is hope, real hope. After being closed for three years, early in 2007 Fleetwood Pier was bought by singer and 'adult' comedian Joey Blower – real name Mike Simmons – through his development company Sirenis Developments Ltd. 'Pal' Joey is no stranger to piers – in fact he works on one! Blower has had a regular show on the nearby Blackpool North Pier – the nearest one to Fleetwood – for several years. Blower candidly (and correctly) calls Fleetwood Pier (his own pier) as 'the worst pier I've ever seen'. Now he hopes to put that right. But, as always, there is a catch.

The only way to save the pier, according to Blower, is to replace the amusement arcade, pub and nightclub with private apartments. This has led to a petition to 'Save the Pier – and keep the amusements'. But for the second part, Blower would have signed it. 'Fleetwood Pier hasn't traded for three years, and even after spending two million on it, the previous owners couldn't make it pay. As the town is now, Fleetwood can't support the pier facilities as they were. It's just not on,' he says. At the time of writing, Blower was undecided whether to re-open the pier deck and pier head to public access, or retain and renovate the structure for the exclusive use of the people living in the new apartments. Now there's a selling-point for estate agents: buy an apartment with your own private pier attached!

Built in 1910, the Fleetwood Victoria pier was built at the end of the 'golden age' of pier building which started in 1860 and lasted fifty years. Fleetwood pier was built by a company set up in 1909 with £30,000-worth of capital. The 492-foot pier, with a landing jetty opened for business on Whit Monday,1910. A pavilion was added in 1911, and there were further improvements in 1930 and 1938. The town had been slow off the mark to join the pier boom. The railway from Preston to Fleetwood was completed in 1840, and in 1844 the *Preston Chronicle* reported that 'cheap trains and pleasure excursions are now all the go and fashion'. But an application for a pier in 1892 brought objections.

Oh, you are ugly! (author's collection)

The decking was replaced in 1946, and the next year a projection room was built to show feature films. On 25 August 1952 the cinema caught alight and the whole pier was wrecked by a huge fire that could be seen 20 miles away. Fleetwood pier was left as a tangle of twisted metal and charred timbers. It was re-built and re-launched as the 'New Super Pier' in 1953. In 1972 the pier had a £70,000 facelift. A new entertainment complex opened on Thursday, 11 December 2003 under new owners. They spent £2 million on the pier, but put it up for sale in June 2006. A bid of £1.2 million was turned down. Fleetwood Pier was again offered for sale by auction in February 2007, but failed to reach its reserve price. This time the highest bid was just £490,000. Now the plans by owner Joey Blower to built apartments on the pier seem to be the only way forward.

Walk a little way along Fleetwood's extensive promenade and you can enjoy the magnificent curved façade of the North Euston Hotel – so called, one presumes, because Londoners had to catch the train from Euston to get here. Further round you encounter the tram and bus terminus and the ferry to Knott End. Best ignore the ferry's multi-coloured timetable (most confusing to my simple mind) – check the chalkboard to ensure that there is a return trip at the time you require. Any miscalculation, and you could be left stranded on the wrong side of the creek. But there are worse things than being stranded in Knott End.

By the way, who is this Joey Blower who has bought the derelict Fleetwood Victoria Pier? You may well ask. To quote his own publicity: 'Joey Blower is one of the world's favourite entertainers, his songs are played all over the world and include such hits as *You Fat Bast**d*, *Yogi Bear*, *White Socks* and of course Joey's own England song, *Glory Glory England*! Joey Blower is without doubt a legend in the world of entertainment.' If Blower does his stuff, he could get another tag: 'the man who saved Fleetwood Pier.'

As you approach the town, the brown tourist-guide signs indicate the pier with a suitable logo. What a pity it would be if the pier disappeared and those signs had to be taken down!

FLEETWOOD VICTORIA

CHRIS'S VERDICT: sad, neglected, ugly, closed – the end is surely nigh, unless …
WALK TIME: n/a

Work started: 1909
First opened: 1910
Designer: G T Lumb (his only pier)
Construction: iron columns, steel bracing, and timber; concrete pier head
Original length: 492 ft (150 m)
Present lenght: 415 ft (127 m)
Fire: 1952
Restoration: 1930, 1938, 1946, 1953, 1972, 2003
Legal: Fleetwood Victoria Pier Order 1907
Original owners: Fleetwood Victoria Pier Co.
Present owners: Sirenis Developments Ltd.
Support group: Save Our Pier petition

Websites: www.engineering-timelines.com, www.joeyblower.com

GRAVESEND TOWN

GRAVESEND TOWN

A beauty by the Thames (author's collection)

WORLD'S OLDEST CAST IRON PIER

Gravesend Town Pier in Kent is on the south side of the Thames estuary. It is the oldest remaining cast iron pier in the world. Recently refurbished and with new facilities on board, it definitely qualifies as a 'seaside' pleasure pier as much as its big brother Southend across the water. Designed by William Tiernwey Clark in 1834 and built as a ferry terminal, the Town Pier is constructed on the site of the original Town Quay which is mentioned in the *Domesday Book* of 1086. It replaced an old pier destroyed by rioting watermen.

A document dated 1293 refers to fining watermen for over-charging. In 1401, a royal charter gave the sole right to the men of Gravesend to operate the 'long ferry' service to and from London. The 'cross ferry' went to Tilbury. Various types of boat were used: the Gravesend barge, tilt boats, wherries and peter boats. The fastest were the tilt boats, open apart from a canvas cover for the passengers. In 1540 there was a causeway from the *Three Crowns* pub for boats and passengers to land.

Paddle steamers started operating on the Thames in the 1830s. The Gravesend Town Pier was one of a number of piers in the area in use during the Victorian era, a time when the town was a popular tourist attraction, with bathing machines on the foreshore. In 1854 the newly-formed London, Tilbury & Southend Railway was given powers to run steamboats between Tilbury on the north bank and Gravesend. The Town Pier was altered to accommodate bigger passenger boats. A new landing stage and terminus station to serve the ferry was opened at Tilbury on 16 May 1930. This station closed on 28 November 1992, but the Tilbury-Gravesend ferry service has been able to carry on thanks to subsidies from both sides of the Thames.

Gravesend Town Pier still looks much as it did when it was built. The building that covers most of the deck is new, but very much in keeping with the pier's original appearance and character. The pier was restored in 2002 and the top remodelled the following year. The restoration was completed by pier owners Gravesham Borough Council with funding assistance from the Heritage Lottery Fund, English Heritage, Kent County Council, SEEDA (South East England Development Agency) and the Manifold Trust. The pier's restoration won the council the silver medal from The Queen's Golden Jubilee Green Apple awards in 2002. The scheme gained the council second place in the 2004 River Thames Society annual award. The Town pier was runner-up in the National Piers Society 2005 Peter Mason Awards for engineering excellence. Morton Partnership were the structural engineers.

After attracting 'huge numbers' of visitors when it re-opened, originally on Saturdays only, under Gravesham Borough Council and Gravesend Space Management the pier was open six days a week, from Monday to Saturday, while refurbishment continued with the construction of a new restaurant at the river end, with panoramic views of the River Thames. The council has entered into a lease with Q Breweries, a local company, to run the bar and restaurant. The bar is now up and running and it was expected that the restaurant would be open by the end of 2007. Public access was then to be restored along the eastern side of the pier.

The pier has a fine clock tower. There are two much bigger clock towers in the town, one on the local church, so which is responsible for the hourly chimes I just couldn't tell.

Gravesend Town Pier, new entrance (courtesy of Gravesham Borough Council)

CHRIS'S VERDICT: fine restoration of a great public asset
WALK TIME: 29 sec (part)

Status: Grade II*
First opened: 1834
Designer: William Tiernwey Clark
Construction: circular cast iron columns, wooden deck
Original length: 260 ft (79 m)
Present length: 260 ft (79 m)
Restoration: 1854, 2002/3 to date
Present owners: Gravesham Borough Council
Websites: www.gravesham.gov.uk, www.riverthames.co.uk

GREAT YARMOUTH BRITANNIA

Britannia Pier fire, 1914 (courtesy of the National Piers Society)

SURVIVOR OF MULTIPLE FIRES

If you want entertainment and amusement, the Britannia Pier is the place to be. The whole of the pier is devoted to these enjoyable pastimes. There is the fun fair and the Pier Theatre and lots, lots more. The Britannia Pier claims to be 'Great Yarmouth's No. 1 Pier', and it's certainly well-maintained with new timbers in the deck.

There have been two Britannia piers. The first, 700 feet long, was opened on 13 July 1858, five years after its neighbour and rival, the Wellington, which was (apparently) exactly the same length. This wooden structure cost £3,158 11s. 6d. Only next year the Britannia Pier suffered a ship collision, the schooner *James & Jessie* reduced the pier by 50 feet. Storm damage in 1868 further reduced the length of the pier, and in 1899 it was demolished. Work on a new pier started in December of that year and, in 1901, the new pier was opened with a temporary pavilion. This was replaced by the first 2,000-seat pier head 'Grand Pavilion' which opened on 21 June 1902 only to be burned down on 22 December 1909. A second 1,200-seat pavilion was built the following year, only for it to be destroyed by fire on 17 April 1914 – allegedly by the Suffragettes who had been refused permission to hold a meeting there. A third pavilion was built with great speed to open on 27 July of the same year.

Fire continued to take its toll as the Floral Hall Ballroom, opened in May 1928, was destroyed on 3 August 1932. A new Grand Ballroom – renamed the Ocean Ballroom in 1947 – was opened in 1933 only for it too to be burned down on 24 April 1954 along with the third pavilion. The pier had been closed and sectioned during World War II but, after being repaired, it was re-opened in 1947. The ballroom was not replaced, but a fourth pavilion was opened on 27 June 1958. At the time of writing, it is still there!

Near the Britannia Pier, there used to be a 145-feet-high 'revolving tower' with a circular platform that went up and down. Admission was 3*d*. In 1952 comedian Norman Evans ('over the garden wall') topped the bill at the pier theatre. On the same bill were Albert & Les Ward, the Maple Leaf Four and the Tiller Girls. The 2006 summer shows featured Basil Brush, Cannon & Ball, Freddie Star, Joe Pasquale, Richard Digance, Jim Davidson and Roy Chubby Brown.

Bold and brash pier entrance
(author's collections)

Britannia Pier, Ocean Ballroom and pavilion in
1953: burned down the following year
(Colin Tooke collection)

Grand Variety Company at the pier pavillion,
c.1905
(courtesy of Northern Writers)

Britannia Pier, July 1909: first pavilion just before
it burned down in December of that year
(Colin Tooke collection)

CHRIS'S VERDICT: ideal for family fun
WALK TIME: 2 min 21 sec

Status: Grade II
Work started: (i) 1857; (ii) 13 December 1900
First opened: (i) 13 July 1858; (ii) 1901 (temporary), 21 June 1902
Designer: (i) A W Morant (his only pier); (ii) James & Arthur Mayoh
Contractor: (ii) Mayoh & Haley, Widnes Foundry Co.
Construction: pier neck, 104 screw piles supporting steelwork ; pier head 200 karri wood piles
Original length: (i) 700 ft (153 m); (ii) 810 ft (168 m)
Storm damage: (i) 1868
Ship collisions: (i) 1859
Fire: 1909, 1914, 1932, 1954
Restoration: 1901/02, 1910, 1914, 1933, 1946/7, 1957/8
Legal: Great Yarmouth New Britannia Pier Act & Order 1899 & 1952
Present owners: Family Amusements Ltd.
Website: www.britannies-pier.co.uk

GREAT YARMOUTH WELLINGTON

Wellington pier front, 2007 (Colin Tooke collection)

NEW LIFE FOR ONE OF OUR OLDEST PIERS

Wellington Pier has a very fine front, a substantial pavilion and an impressive, if somewhat angular, adjoining Winter Gardens, but on my visit that is all I could enjoy. Sadly, the rest of the pier was closed. Hopefully, this will change, but I saw the sea end as completely derelict with huge timbers sticking forlornly out of the sand. The pier neck was classed as a 'development site' and there were signs of improvement with much of the structural members encased in concrete.

Local businessman and twice mayor of the town, Charles John Palmer, was the driving force behind the setting-up of the Great Yarmouth Wellington Pier Company in 1852, the year the Duke of Wellington (the one who defeated Napoleon in the battle of Waterloo, of course) had died. Originally planned some ten years earlier, the Wellington Pier, named after the Iron Duke, opened on 31 October 1853. It was completed only four months after receiving its parliamentary approval. The pier was a wooden structure, 700 feet long and cost £6,776. It had ornamental railings and a 100-foot-long 'promenading platform' at the pier head.

Admission was one penny (old money) for adults and a half penny for children – yet it took the grand total of £581 7*s.* 1*d.* for admissions in its first year. Out of this, the pier company paid 17*s.* 6*d.* to the pier master and 7*s.* 6*d.* to his assistant. Competition from its local rival the Britannia Pier from 1858 reduced the takings, and the company never recovered. However, in 1899, mixed bathing was allowed 'in suitable garments', although men could still bathe nude before 8 a.m. It was said that some ladies would go on an early morning walk along the promenade.

In 1900 the Great Yarmouth Corporation bought the Wellington Pier for £1,250 and rebuilt it with a new seaward-end art nouveau pavilion which opened on 13 July 1903, along with pier gardens and a bandstand. When military band concerts lost their popular appeal, the area became an outdoor skating rink. Also in the 1900s, the Corporation paid £2,400 for the Winter Gardens at Torquay, dismantled it and transported the whole lot from Devon, rebuilding it at the shore end of the Wellington Pier.

In the first half of the twentieth century, the Wellington Pier provided a variety of entertainment: concerts, variety shows, firework displays, speedboat trips, whist drives, roller skating, boxing, indoor bowls, miniature golf, dancing and children's races. In 1930 a whiskey firm put up a large electric cricket scoreboard in the pier gardens for the test match series between England and Australia. The Pier pavilion was affectionately known by artistes as 'the Cow Shed' due to its tarred, rustic roof and glass-topped partition walls. As the dressing room windows were conveniently located facing the sea, hard-up performers would cast their fishing lines before a show and haul them in at the interval!

After conducting the Wellington Pier Orchestra, Henry Wallace Hartley took over the orchestra on the liner *Mauretania*. Much-loved actress Dora Bryan was a dancer at the pier theatre before World War II, when diminutive comedian and entertainer Arthur Askey also performed. In the 1950s it was the Ronnie Ronalde Show, and Bill Pertwee appeared with the Beverley Sisters in the Gorleston Pavilion. Comedian Jimmy Cricket had his first summer season at the Wellington Pier in 1982, but the most enduring entertainer has been comedian Jim Davidson who appeared here for 15 years in succession. For some years, he just happened to be running the theatre!

The sea end of Wellington Pier was rebuilt in 1971 at a cost of £30,000, but by 1986 the council was considering demolishing the whole structure after being told it would cost £1 million to put it right. There was a public outcry and the council eventually decided to put the pier out to lease. Davidson took this on in 1996. He gave up the lease in 2002 when Family Amusements took over. Closed in 2001, pier owners Family Entertainments have rebuilt the former 1500-seat theatre as a

Wellington Pier, original entrance, late 1890s (Colin Tooke collection)

family entertainment centre with bowling alleys, bars, a live entertainment area and restaurant. The pier neck is being replaced in the £2 million restoration scheme.

Currently, the theatre remains closed but the Victorian Winter Gardens – now 'Jim Davidson's Winter Gardens' – which were refurbished during 2002, and in June 2003, exactly 150 years after work started on building the pier – are where the first phase of the pier's redevelopment began. The Wellington pier re-opened for the 2004 season on 3 April. The redevelopment is planned to continue with the rebuilding of the pier itself which will incorporate a state-of-the-art tenpin bowling centre. Both Yarmouth piers overlook Scroby Sands wind farm.

Wellington Pier, 1903 pavilion, Winter Gardens, south lawn and bandstand, 1930
(Colin Tooke collection)

CHRIS'S VERDICT: a sad sight, but there is hope for the future
WALK TIME: n/a

Work started: June 1853
First opened: 31 October 1853
Designer: Peter Ashcroft (his only pier)
Construction: originally all timber, replaced by steel girders on wooden piles
Original length: 700 ft (212 m)
Present length: 700 ft (212 m)
Restoration: 1901/03, 1971, 2003
Legal: Great Yarmouth Wellington Pier Orders 1901 & 1921
Original owners: Great Yarmouth Wellington Pier Co.
Present owners: Family Amusements Ltd.
Website: www.wellington-pier.co.uk

HASTINGS

A fine pier, but when will it reopen? (author's collection)

WAITING TO BE REBORN

The first ever August Bank Holiday, Monday, 5 August 1872, saw the opening of Hastings Pier, five years after approval was first given by an Act of Parliament. Built to a Birch design, it cost £23,250 and was 910 feet long with a 2,000-seat pavilion at the seaward end. The tollhouse was destroyed in a storm in 1877 but was quickly replaced. A landing stage costing £2,000 was added in 1885. Amusements introduced before World War I included a shooting gallery, 'animated pictures', slot machines, a rifle range, bowling alley and a Viennese Band.

The shore-end building, known as the Parade, was sold to the local council in 1913 to finance a new arcade with shops and a tea room. Fire destroyed the pavilion on 15 July 1917. A new pavilion was built in 1926, and an art deco façade added in the 1930s. The White Rock Pavilion opposite the pier opened in 1927 with the 'Fol-de-Rols', and which, in 1938, included Jack Warner, Arthur Askey and Richard Murdoch. A 1938 storm damaged the seaward end of the pier and its pavilion had to be closed. It was repaired at a cost of £22,000. As well as being sectioned in World War II, the pier also suffered bomb damage. It re-opened in 1946 and two solaria added: the West View in 1951 and the East View in 1956. *The Rolling Stones* played at the pier pavilion in 1964.

A tapestry designed to mark the 900th anniversary of the Battle of Hastings (in 1066, 'as any fule kno') was housed in a specially-built triodome on the parade extension in 1966. In 1968 the council sold the pier and triodome to a private company that converted the triodome into an amusement arcade.

In 1993 Humberglow Ltd. bought Hastings Pier for £196,000 but £100,000 of storm damage occurred the same year. The pier has been up for sale since 1996, but the shore-end pavilion still offers bingo. In June 2006 Hastings Council served a closure notice on the pier owners, using their

Hastings Pier on fire, 1917 (courtesy of the National Piers Society)

Hastings Pier, c.1908 (Frances Foote collection)

emergency powers. The pier closed on Friday 16 June 2006. In 2007 Stylus Sports paid £200,000 for work to be done underneath the former theatre, now a bingo hall, allowing the central section of the pier to re-open for business on Friday, 6 July 2007. The following weekend, lightning struck the pier, 200 people had to be evacuated and the pier was temporarily re-closed.

Local supporters are working hard to have the pier restored. The series of buildings of different eras along most of its length give Hastings Pier its unique appearance. Meantime, not only are you unable to walk on the pier, you are also barred from walking under it due to 'danger of falling debris'.

CHRIS'S VERDICT: a fine pier well worth restoring
WALK TIME: n/a

Status: Grade II
Work started: December 1869
First opened: 1872
Designer: Eugenius Birch
Contractor: R Laidlaw
Construction: cast iron columns on screw piles, lattice-girder iron frame, wood deck
Original length: 910 ft (278 m)
Present length: 910 ft (278 m)
Storm damage: 1877, 1938, 1993
Ship collisions: 1873, 1884, 1940
Fire: 1917
Restoration: 1885, 1910–12, 1926, 1930s, 1950s, 1969
Legal: Hastings Pier Acts & Orders 1867–1937
Present owners: Ravenclaw Investments
Support group: Hastings Pier Consortium
Websites: www.hastings.gov.uk, www2.hastingstoday.co.uk

HERNE BAY

Herne Bay pier head, c.1910 (Mike Bundock collection)

IT'S NOT AN ISLAND – IT'S THE END OF THE PIER!

No, it is not an island out there in the Thames Estuary – it is the old pier head, separated by a thousand yards or more of water from the surviving remains of what was our third longest pier. The shore end is well-maintained, and the stone-built entrance is impressive if not imposing. The pier pavilion is unusual in that it is a sports pavilion, home of England roller-hockey champions Herne Bay United. Its metal cladding is wearing well. The centre caters for several sports, 'keep fit' and kids' activities.

Herne Bay Pier has had three incarnations. The first in 1832 was a wooden pier 3,633 feet long, by far the longest at that time. It cost a massive £50,000. This wooden structure was designed by Thomas Telford and built by local carpenter Thomas Rhodes. It was said that Rhodes did most of the design work, his drawings counter-signed by Telford who took the credit. The wooden pier suffered the depredations of the Teredo worm as well as storm damage. Steamer services from London ceased in 1862. The pier was closed, and eventually dismantled and sold for scrap in 1871. Remarkably, a sail-powered carriage operated on its baggage line. It made its maiden 'voyage' along the pier on 13 June 1833. The first Herne Bay Pier Co. went into liquidation in 1870, and the following year the Herne Bay Improvement Commissioners bought the approach to the pier for £100 and the promenade for £250.

The second pier was a far more modest: a 320-feet wood and iron affair, at a suitably modest cost of £2,000. It was opened on 27 August 1873 by the Lord Mayor of London, Sir Sydney Waterlow. A theatre was added in 1884. From 1896 to 1899 a new iron pier, incorporating the second pier, was built to a length of 3,787 feet with an electric railway. Open to the public from Easter 1899, it was opened officially on 14 September of that year when 3,787 visitors paid to tread the boards. It

Impressive front office (author's collection)

was then the second-longest in the country (to Southport, then 4,380 feet long) and had cost £60,000 to build and fit out. The pier company went into liquidation and builders Head Wrightson took over the pier before selling it on to the local council in 1909.

Tragedy struck on the electric traction tramway on Tuesday, 16 July 1901. The luggage trolley left the track, and both the driver and conductor, along with two passengers, leapt out but failed to apply the brakes. The driving trailer went through the pier rails and into the sea. One elderly lady was killed. Surprisingly, the coroner's verdict stated 'that no blame could be attached to anyone'. On another occasion, after World War I when the pier train ran into the sea, professional diver *Professor* Bert Powsey saved several people from drowning. One woman he saved gave him a shilling as a reward.

Herne Bay Pier, c.1905 (Frances Foote collection)

Herne Bay Pier theatre fire, 9 September 1928 (Mike Bundock collection)

World War I put a temporary end to steamer services. The tramcars became shelters and were later sold for scrap. The trams resumed in 1925 with a petrol-driven service, to be replaced in turn by battery-driven ones ten years later. The service closed for good on 3 November 1939.

In February 1904 Henry C Jones, managing director of the pier company, was arrested on charges of embezzling funds on behalf of the pier from Holbourne Borough Council, of which he was treasurer. Jones was jailed for five years and the pier company went in receivership. In 1909 the receiver sold the pier to Herne Bay Urban District Council for £6,000. A competition for the design of the Grand Pier Pavilion in 1910 was won by Percy Waldram and built for £2,000.

The old pier theatre and entrance shops burned down on 9 September 1928. A new entrance was completed four years later. During World War

II, the pavilion was turned into a factory for making camouflage netting. The pier was sectioned but later repaired. A Wellington bomber crashed into the sea close to the pier on 27 November 1941. After the war, the council received £21,924 15s. 1d. in war damage compensation. (I wonder what the penny was for?) Steamer services resumed in 1947.

The pier entrance was damaged by heavy seas on 1 March 1949. In 1950 the pier tram was sold off for scrap, fetching £12 10s. During the night of 31 January–1 February 1953, the pier entrance was damaged by a storm surge. The stone balustarding, which had originally come from Old London Bridge, was broken down and subsequently replaced by iron railings. In the winter of 1962/3, the sea froze around the whole length of the pier for several weeks. The steamer service ended in 1963.

In September 1968 insurance cover on the pier north of the pavilion was withdrawn, and the pier deck was closed to the public. In June 1970 the shore-end Grand Pavilion, which opened in 1910, was destroyed by fire. Former Prime Minister Edward Heath opened a new £900,000 sports pavilion on 5 September 1976. On 11 January 1978 a huge storm destroyed much of the remaining part of the pier neck, leaving the pier head isolated out at sea. More of it collapsed in the storms of January and February 1979. The last few pieces were removed in 1980, leaving the pier head in splendid isolation.

The remaining short neck leading to the pavilion has a central shelter and seats, and there is a walkway on both sides of the sports centre. If you find the pier too short for a stroll, you can walk along the adjacent Neptune's Arm with the bonus of being able to take in the pier and the views from the viewing platform at the end. But all this could change. There is a proposal to extend the pier all the way out to the old pier head. The cost? A mere £12 million. In 2007 moves were underway to set up a trust and apply for grant funding.

Herne Bay Pier. J & F Harwood engraving, June 1841 (Mike Bundock collection)

CHRIS'S VERDICT: imagine walking to the pier head!
WALK TIME: 1 min 18 sec

Work started: (i) 1831; (ii); 1873; (iii)1896
First opened: (i) 1832; (ii) 27 August 1873; (iii) 14 September 1899
Designer: (i) Thomas Telford and Thomas Rhodes (their only pier); (ii) Wilkinson and Smith (their only pier); (iii) E Mattheson (his only pier).
Contractor: (i) Thomas Rhodes, (iii) Head Wrightson, Stockton-on-Tees
Construction: (i) timber; (ii) wood and iron; (iii) iron piles, steel supports, timber deck
Original length: (i) 3633 ft (1108 m): (ii) 320 ft (98 m); (iii) 3787 ft (1155 m)
Present length: 320 ft (98 m)
Storm damage: 1860s, 1953, 1978
Fire: 1928, 1970
Restoration: 1873, 1896-99, 1946, 1976
Original owners: Herne Bay Promenade Pier Co.
Legal: Herne Bay Pier Orders 1891, 1895, 1952
Present owners: Canterbury City Council
Website: www.hernebaypier.co.uk

HYTHE

Pier head station. Spacious waiting room on right (author's collection)

A STEP BACK IN HISTORY

There has been a ferry service from Hythe to Southampton 'since time immemorial' says the blurb on this very well used pier. The 'Hithe Ferye' is shown on Saxton's 1575 map of Hampshire, and that was in the days of Good Queen Bess (Elizabeth I). Yet Hythe Pier and its wonderful, wonderful pier train are very much part of modern living. Hundreds of commuters use these facilities, along with the excellent ferry service, every working day.

Once over, passengers were rowed across Southampton Water in wherries that could carry up to ten passengers. From 1852 the wherrymen were licensed and had to wear a brass disc showing their official licence number on an armband, much like taxi-drivers today. Before Hythe Pier was built, passengers who did not want to get their feet wet had to be carried ashore, no doubt earning an extra tip for the wherryman.

As well as trippers and commuters, the great and the good have also patronised Hythe Pier. Before World War I, King Alfonso XIII of Spain (that's Alfonso the thirteenth, unlucky for some, he abdicated in 1931), Kaiser Wilhelm II of Germany, Princess Beatrice of Battenberg and Prince and Princess Henry of Prussia. Just before D-Day in June 1944, King George V took the train along the pier. Alfonso 'ambled along the pier to a thunderous ovation'. The Hythe ferry *Carrick Lass* was called up to do duty in World War II but was lost at sea in 1940.

Now about this train. Originally sited at the Avonmouth Mustard Gas Factory in World War I, this unique set of tiny electric locos and rolling stock came to Hythe Pier in July 1922, adapting a 24-inch gauge baggage line installed in 1909. Apart from running repairs, both engines and carriages are as original and very fine they are too. The Hythe Pier train vies with its rival across the water, the Ryde Pier train (*qv*). Both claim to be the most reliable train in the UK, with ninety-nine point something per cent reliability. But there is a flaw in the argument somewhere, at least as far as Hythe is concerned. I know for a fact that the driver of the Hythe train deliberately slows down when he sees the ferry is slightly delayed. His philosophy is that the passengers get restless if the train stops, but they're ok as long as it keeps moving.

There is one record the Hythe train definitely keeps for itself: the oldest continually operating pier train (since July 1922). While other piers were sectioned, Hythe Pier and its train were pressed into war service during World War II. There is a flat wagon in front of the train for your cases and rucksacks. The three carriages – taking 48 passengers – are cosy and cramped, but that's half the fun. And it is only a three-minute ride. The train runs 364 days a year, every day except Christmas day, clocking up a grand total of 430,000 passenger journeys per annum. Maximum speed is 10 mph. A transformer provides the 220 dc current that drives the train via a 3.5 hp motor built by Brush Electrical Engineering Co.

It is a remarkably busy train, for a little 'un. It runs every half hour from 6 a.m. to midnight three days a week, 6 a.m. to 8 p.m. three days, and 9–6 on Sundays. At 700 yards each trip, I reckon that's 83.5 miles a week: 4,343 miles a year. In 85 years, this train has run a total of 369,070 miles, that's almost 15 times around the world! As well as a spare carriage, there is a spare loco. Just as well.

Hythe Pier advertises boat trips, train rides and great views. That is plenty for any pier enthusiast, but there is nothing more. There are no amusements whatsoever, but the pedestrianised High Street, full of character, is just a few steps from the pier entrance. But you can still have fun on Hythe Pier. On 21 June 1998, over 100 people line-danced on the pier. There is a photograph to prove it. The pier head was being renewed in 2007 and hopefully will provide much more seating, but for the leg-weary there is a commodious waiting room serving the sea-end station and ferry terminal. There are

Hythe Pier train, c.1930 (courtesy of White Horse Ferries)

only a couple of seats at the land end station, but you can always wait on the train. For your 80 pence toll you can walk the pier or ride the train, or both – one way each way, of course.

Walking or riding, there are great views all round from this unspoiled pier. Southampton Water is always busy with ships of every description. You could be lucky enough to see the *Queen Mary II* or *Queen Elizabeth II* when they visit their home port – check the dates on the Hythe Ferry website. The doomed *Titanic* set sail from a nearby berth on 10 April 1912. For 40 years, you could watch flying boats taking off and landing. The first passenger services using these romantic aeroplanes

That wonderful pier train! (author's collection)

The White Star liner RMS Olympic, *sister ship of the* Titanic, *passing Hythe Pier, c.1930. When she was built in 1911, the* Olympic *was the largest ship in existence. She went to the aid of the stricken* Titanic *in 1912, and lasted until 1935 (courtesy of White Horse Ferries)*

began in 1919, the last was in 1958. Racing flying boats, built by the Supermarine Company close to the pier, won the Schneider Trophy four times in the 1920s and 1930s. They also built Spitfire aircraft, designed by R J Mitchell. Hovercraft inventor Sir Christopher Cockerill lived in Hythe and used the pier, as did T E Lawrence (*Lawrence of Arabia*).

R.N. Commandos were billeted in the town of Hythe prior to embarkation for Normandy from Hythe Pier. A Memorial Stone is situated in a small park close to Hythe Pier. The stone was erected by the town's folk to commemorate the event.

The very solid longitudinal planking on Hythe Pier is made from Ekki wood, 'from a well-respected and managed renewable source,' we are assured. If you want to help Hythe Pier, you can always purchase a plank. 'After all,' reads the blurb, 'timber decking doesn't grow on trees'. The planks are fixed with stainless steel coach bolts, not the usual six-inch nails which can rust and 'blow'. The pier lights are somewhat utilitarian but do not detract from the pier's unspoiled looks.

Take care when walking the pier with young children or animals – there is only a plain three-bar rail between you and the water, and the live rail that powers the train. Old photographs and information boards along the pier add to the experience. You can see the very spot where, on the evening of Saturday, 1 November 2003, the MV *Donald Redford* completely severed the pier, leaving a 150-foot gap. The pier was re-opened on Wednesday, 7 January 2004 by Ted Vaughan, chairman of the Hythe Ferry Users Group. That is commuter power for you. The boat trip to Southampton takes only 12 minutes.

Hythe Pier was a long time coming. Plans drawn up in 1870 came to nothing. Work eventually started in 1878, and the last pile was driven on 29 June 1880. The 2,100 feet pier was opened on New Year's Day 1881. In 1894 Hythe Sailing Club built a clubhouse on the pier head. A baggage line, added in 1909, was adapted to carry passengers after World War I. A new 24-inch gauge tramway opened in July 1922. The same Brush locos operate on the line today. Since World War II, the pier has been well-maintained. A pontoon erected in the 1930s was moved to the pier head in 1947. In the 1960s, the entrance was modernised and the shelters removed from the deck. The pier head building was developed in 1970/1. The pier head timber deck was replaced in 1982, and sub-structure repairs costing £290,000 were made in 1987/8. This included replacing trusses on the inshore and middle sections.

Diving from the pier head, c.1920 (courtesy of White Horse Ferries)

CHRIS'S VERDICT: combines beauty with utility, plus its wonderful train. My favourite pier
WALK TIME: 6 min 11 sec

Work started: 1878
First opened: 1 January 1881
Designer: J Wright (his only pier)
Construction: pairs of cast iron piles with cross bracing, steelwork supporting timber deck
Original length: 2100 ft (640 m)
Present length: 2100 ft (640 m)
Ship collisions: 2003
Restoration: 1896, 1947, 1960s, 1970/1, 1982, 1987/8
Original owners: Hythe Pier Order 1878
Present owners: White Horse Ferries Ltd.
Pier of the Year: 1999
Website: www.hythe-ferry.co.uk

LLANDUDNO

Standing proud: pier head pavilion (author's collection)

'Y' THIS PIER IS UNIQUE

Llandudno Pier in Gwynedd on the North Wales coast is y-shaped, with the 'y' at the land end, so it is a pier in two parts. Llandudno Pier is also the longest in Wales, and the fifth longest in the UK. From the promenade, the extension that runs past the Grand Hotel has a great variety of shops, stalls and amusements. Just behind you can see the gaunt remains of the shore-end pavilion, destroyed by fire on 13 February 1994. Past the Grand Hotel, you are on to the pier proper with another entrance close to the happily named Happy Valley car park. From there to the pier head is a well-preserved example of a Victorian pier with its handsome cabins, seating and fine balustrading, and cast iron lampposts.

I was delighted to be told that my *bête noir* – those big, black litter-bins – were to be replaced in 2008 by something far more authentic and fitting for this Victorian masterpiece. At the pier head there are three fine and original buildings, a bar and a café on either side of the Penny Arcade, which in fact houses only modern machines. The main pavilion with its striking dome still carries traces of its original decoration. As well as the enjoyment of the pier itself; the views all around are stunning.

A landing stage at Llandudno called St George's Jetty lasted from 1857 to 1876, when it suffered storm damage and was demolished. Work on a new iron pier started almost immediately and the present pier was opened in August 1877. It was 1,234 feet (376 m) long and had a bandstand at the seaward end. In 1884 the shoreward end and pavilion were completed, extending the pier – landwards as it were – to 2,295 feet (700 m). The landing stage was built in 1891 and reinforced in 1904. In 1905 the sea-end bandstand was replaced by a pier-head pavilion.

In 1935 'What the butler saw' machines on the pier offered such attractions as 'Her Hubby's Sweetie', 'Keep Cool' and 'That Boy on Palm Beach' – the videos of days gone by! During World

Pier head, c.1914 – the Grand Hotel is on the left
(Frances Foote collection)

Llandudno Pier, c.1911
(courtesy of the National Piers Society)

It's like painting the Forth Bridge! Pier maintenance is
never-ending, especially with these fancy railings
(author's collection)

Steamer at Llandudno Pier, showing the pier's two land-
ward 'arms' (Llandudno Enthusiast collection)

Boarding the pier (Llandudno Enthusiast collection)

War II the pier was used for 'Dad's Army' Home Guard training. The present steel and concrete landing stage was built in 1969. After having a £70,000 refurbishment in 1984/5, the 2,000-seat shore-end pavilion with its decorated spandrels and iron stairs was burned down in a 1994 fire.

It is noted on the pier that Sir Malcolm Sargent (1895–1967), the world-famous orchestra conductor, stared his early career at the pier pavilion. In 1926 he was invited to take over the Llandudno Pier Orchestra. He stayed for two seasons before going on to even greater triumphs. Sir Malcolm, in due course, became conductor of the Halle Orchestra (1939), the Liverpool Philharmonic (1942), and the BBC Symphony Orchestra (1950–57), and he was chief conductor of the Henry Wood Promenade Concerts for many years. Knighted in 1947, Sir Malcolm died in London in 1967. So, playing on the pier is not a bad place to start! In his youth, composer Malcolm Arnold played trumpet in the resident Llandudno Pier Orchestra. He went on to compose nine symphonies and thirty concertos. Arnold was also a prolific film composer. He wrote the music for the 1957 film *Bridge on the River Kwai* which won him an Oscar. Sir Malcolm Arnold died in 2006.

CHRIS'S VERDICT: near perfect
WALK TIME: 5 min 04 sec (full length)

Status: Grade II*
Work started: June 1876
First opened: August 1877
Designer: James Brunlees
Construction: braced cast iron columns, steel and concrete landing stage
Original length: (i) 1234 ft (376 m); (ii) 2295 ft (700 m), 1884
Present length: 2295 ft (700 m)
Ship collisions: 1907
Fire: 1994
Restoration: 1884, 1891, 1904/05, 1938, 1984/5
Present owner: Six Piers Ltd.
Support group: Llandudno Enthusiasts
Pier of the Year: 2005
Websites: www.llandudno-forum.co.uk, www.olle.co.uk

LOWESTOFT CLAREMONT

Claremont pier deck, c.1911 (courtesy of the National Piers Society)

RESCUE BID AWAITED

Gazing forlornly through the wire netting that keeps the public off the deck of Lowestoft Claremont Pier, all one can do is imagine what the Claremont was like in its heyday, and what it could be like if funding can be found to restore it. But the Claremont needs a lot of work. The decking is still there and looks in fairly good nick, but there are no seats, no shelters and all of the balustrading is gone. The shore end facilities are fine and there is ample parking in front of the pier. But that's all.

Despite the Claremont being much the younger of Lowestoft's two piers, its supporters claim it to be the town's only *real* pier. 'Lowestoft South Pier', they allege, 'is not a "proper pier" as it's really a sort of harbour wall'. But the South Pier is recognised as such by the National Piers Society, and that is what really counts. Talk about rival football supporters!

One of three east coast piers built by the Coast Development Co. (CDC) primarily to serve its steamship business, Lowestoft Claremont Pier was ideal for the purpose because the whole length of the pier (670 feet) was in water deep enough for ships to berth. The CDC, formed in 1898, also built Felixstowe and Southwold piers. The company operated the famous *Belle* steamers from London Bridge, with trips to Southend, Clacton, Walton-on-the-Naze, Great Yarmouth and Lowestoft, which had also benefited from the rail link with Great Yarmouth.

Built over half a century after its neighbour, Lowestoft South Pier, the Claremont Pier was a 600 foot-long wooden construction when it was first opened in 1903. In 1912 the T-shaped pier head was extended and a new pavilion built, extending the pier to 760 feet. The original wooden piles were renewed using greenheart timber. The steamer service continued until 1939 when the pier was closed due to World War II. As an east coast pier facing the threat of invasion, the Claremont Pier

Lots of under-cover amusement (author's collection)

There's a lot to do to restore this pier deck (author's collection)

was sectioned. Later the gap was closed with a Bailey Bridge. The Army kept the pier as a training centre until 1948.

Abandoned and derelict, in 1949 the Claremont pier was taken over by actor and pipe-smoker George Studd after Lowestoft Town Council had turned down the chance to buy it for £4,000. By 1950 Mr Studd had built a reinforced concrete platform and a new pavilion, but in 1962 storms took away the T-shaped head and the pier was reduced to its present length of 720 feet.

While the shore end of the pier was renovated in the 1980s, the rest of the pier, sadly, remained closed on safety grounds. Rescue plans came to naught. With new piles needed and the decking requiring replacement, refurbishment costs are high. The Claremont ('ideal for commercial development') has been advertised for sale at £2.8 million! 'Serious enquiries only' should be directed to 07917 202 592.

In 2000 Lowestoft Council commissioned artist David Ward to create a visual link between Lowestoft's two piers. Ward's *St Elmo's Fire* installation was unveiled in the spring of 2001. Halfway along Claremont Pier, you will see a group of lights suspended from tall poles. The lights, randomly controlled by computer, are reflected on the water between the two piers. The intensity of the reflections depends entirely on meteorological conditions.

CHRIS'S VERDICT: crying out for restoration
WALK TIME: n/a

Work started: 1902
First opened: 1903
Designer: D J Fox (his only pier)
Contractor: J Trueman
Construction: wooden piles, replaced by greenheart timber (1913); reinforced concrete platform (1950)
Original length: 600 ft (153 m); 760 ft (230 m), 1913
Present length: 720 ft (220 m)
Storm damage: 1962
Restoration: 1912/13, 1948–50, 1980s
Original owners: The Coast Development Co.
Present owners: Family Amusements Ltd.
Website: www.claremontpierforsale.co.uk

LOWESTOFT SOUTH

South Pier, c.1922 (Frances Foote collection)

WHEN IS A PIER NOT A PIER?

I am sorry, I know this is going to upset some people, but to me Lowestoft South Pier is not a true pier – it is a breakwater enclosing the harbour. Certainly, the South Pier offers everything a pier should – amusements, walking, fine views, sea air and fishing, but it is not 'walking on water'. But who am I to argue with the National Piers Society? And the South Pier Family Entertainment Centre claims to be 'Suffolk's most popular tourist attraction!' So you pays your money and you takes your choice, as my old maths master used to say. There has always been a separate admission charge for this pier, indicating its entertainment function. In the 1970s it was still only a penny, the lowest pier entry fee in the country. Entry is now free.

You can drive onto the pier, but then you miss the pleasure of walking past the marina with its sleek and expensive pleasure craft. Just how often do these yachts and cruisers actually go out to sea, I wonder? I would bet that many of them hardly ever venture out of the harbour, but no doubt provide much pleasure for their owners nevertheless. There are plenty of other things to see as you look across the harbour, not least of which is a giant wind turbine that I saw turning at a very impressive pace. Huge modules are being built for the North Sea oil and gas industry, and there are plenty of other harbour activities.

Look the other way and you have fine views along the shore to the Claremont Pier and beyond. At night there's the *St Elmo's Fire* lighting that links the two piers. The granite rocks laid down to dissipate wave action within the pier are as good as any artwork with their irregular angular shapes and their many different colours. Moored alongside the pier is the historic trawler *Mincarlo* LT412, manned by volunteers. Admission is free, but under-18s must be accompanied by an adult. At the far end of the South Pier and its companion the North Pier are two of the smallest lighthouses I've ever seen, but they seem to be accessible for maintaining the harbour lights.

Aberystwyth Royal – cut short

Bangor Garth – a real beauty

Beaumaris – crab fishing, the best in town

Blackpool Central – it's all fun!

Blackpool North – classic seaside pier

Blackpool South – swinging over the waves

Bognor Regis – was home of the Birdman Rally

Boscombe – rebuilding, 2007

Bournemouth – up to date

Brighton Palace – Brighton Rocks!

Brighton West – this great pier will surely rise again

Burnham-on-Sea – as it was built

Clacton – full of fun

Cleethorpes – shortest actual pier

Clevedon – delicate tracery

Colwyn Bay Victoria – defying the odds

Cromer – eye delight

Deal – a great deal of pleasure

Eastbourne – shining example

Falmouth Prince of Wales – pretty as a picture

Felixstowe – restoration awaited

Fleetwood Victoria – can Joey save it?

Gravesend Town – a real pleasure

Great Yarmouth Britannia – the great survivor

Great Yarmouth Wellington – redevelopment under way

Hastings – hope for the future

Herne Bay – missing the bit in the middle

Hythe – iconic pier train

Llandudno – enduring classic

Lowestoft Claremont – on the edge

Lowestoft South – pier with no legs

Mumbles – near pier-fect

Paignton – plenty to offer

Penarth – class throughout

Ramsey Queens –
must not die

Ryde – underground,
overground, over the sea

St Annes – well maintained

Saltburn – sheer simplicity

Sandown Culver –
simply fun

Skegness – something old, something new

Southend-on-Sea – pier train "Sir John Betjeman" heads out

Southport – behind "Funland" lies Britain's second-longest seaside pier

Southsea Clarence – funfair with pier attached

Southsea South Parade – the pier that rocked

Southwold – a jolly good time

Swanage – fighting the Gribble Worm

Teignmouth Grand – a grand pier indeed

Torquay Princess – piggyback pier

Totland Bay –
artist's paradise

Walton-on-the-Naze –
a good walk

Weston-super-Mare
Birnbeck –
needs a miracle

Weston-super-Mare Grand –
lives up to its name

*Weymouth Commercial/Pleasure –
great views all round*

*Weymouth Pier Bandstand –
but the bandstand's gone*

Worthing – happy mix of styles

Yarmouth – made for strolling

These photographs were taken by the author when he visited all of the UK seaside piers in 2007.

The harbour wall provides a fine walk
(author's collection)

East Point Pavilion – a mini-Crystal
Palace!
(author's collection)

Lowestoft South Pier, c.1960
(Tim Mickleburgh collection)

South Pier, c.1910
(David Clarke collection)

The very handsome East Point Pavilion, a veritable mini-Crystal Palace, faces the pier entrance across the square where there is one of those fountains that squirts jets of water out of the ground at unexpected intervals. Great for kids of all ages! The pavilion has a café, a roomy Tourist Information Centre and well-maintained toilets. These last are ten pence a time, but beware when exiting – the automatic barriers open inwards and can strike a painful blow.

In 1831 William Cubitt built two 500 feet harbour piers in Lowestoft for the Norwich and Lowestoft Navigation Company. In 1844 Sir Martin Peto formed a new company to improve the harbour, and the 1,320 feet South Pier was built in 1846. A reading room was opened in 1854 and a bandstand jetty in 1884. Both were destroyed by fire in 1885. A new reading room and pavilion were built in 1889–91, but they were damaged during world War II and demolished. In 1928 the pier was strengthened with concrete.

The Duke of Edinburgh, no less, officially opened the rebuilt pavilion on 2 May 1956. The pavilion played host to various big bands: Jimmy Young, Dennis Lotis, Lita Rosa, Craig Douglas and Brian Johnson, amongst others. In an earlier era, Lowestoft's Sparrows Nest Pavilion advertised *The Co-optimists*, which featured the stage artist Stanley Holloway on Sunday, 6 September 1931.

A miniature railway ran along the whole length of the pier. In the 1950s, a new £220,000 leisure centre was built to replace the previous shore-end building. There were further improvements during 1974/5. But in 1987 structural problems forced the closure of the seaward end of the pier. The proposed development of a new Marina and private clubhouse for yacht owners saw the pavilion demolished and the pier closed to the public. The marina scheme never came off, but the pier was re-opened to its full length in June 1993 after the council had spent £30,000 on repairs. Planning improvements in 2006 costing £30,000 included improved lighting, replacing the existing concrete bollards with marine-grade blue-lit stainless steel bollards.

CHRIS'S VERDICT: all a pier should be, apart from having no legs
WALK TIME: 3 min 24 sec

First opened: 1846
Designer: Sir Morton Peto (his only pier)
Original length: 1320 ft (403 m)
Present length: 1320 ft (403 m)
Fire: 1885
Restoration: 1949/50, 1988
Legal: Lowestoft South Pier Orders 1900 & 1912
Present owners: Oulton Broad Leisure Ltd.
Website: www.thesouthpier.co.uk

MUMBLES

A welcome is a welcome in any language (author's collection)

ALL-WEATHER FAMILY FUN

You can park on the approach to Mumbles Pier, but better to drive up to the top of Mumbles Head and park there for great views of the pier and Swansea Bay. There are steps down to the pier with its modern pavilion housing a café, amusement arcade and first-floor bowling alley. There is the Pier Hotel and a skating rink. The shore-side terrace ('probably the best outside terrace in Wales') in front of the pavilion has fancy cast iron railings. There are seats and shelters on the approach.

Everything is well-kept at Mumbles Pier, from the flower-baskets to the unobtrusive litter bins in a gentle brown. The pier itself is largely uncluttered, the only garish features of note are from photo-boards (stick your faces in the holes) and two somewhat grotesque plastic play animals that would be better placed on the forecourt. Although claimed to bring 'a touch of Disneyland' to the pier, to me these two monsters spoil an otherwise classically simply pier deck. Around the head of the pier there are ornate seats; however, the right-hand side is closed for renovation work. There is a two-tier fishing jetty at the end of the pier.

A simple arch over two wooden pay desks invite you onto the pier for a 50 pence toll. The lifeboat station is off at right angles, mid-pier. Fishing is available to all-comers at £3 a day. As well as the views all around Swansea Bay, there are two rocky islets close by, one with a lighthouse and fort. They can be reached on foot at low tide, but this is definitely not recommended. The original Mumbles lighthouse was completed in 1794. Its light came from two coal fires! It was electrified in 1969 and converted to solar power in 1995.

Mumbles Pier was opened on 10 May 1898 and cost £17,000. There were no pavilions, just a bandstand and amusement stalls. It was the terminus for the Swansea and Mumbles Railway, which continued up until 1960. The lifeboat station was added around 1929. The pier was sectioned

Mumbles Pier, c.1930 (Frances Foote collection)

in 1940 but did not re-open until 9 June 1956, with a new landing jetty.. The shore-side amusement arcade was built ten years later. In 1987/8 some of the pier's steelwork was renewed at a cost of £40,000.

In 1998 the landward-end building was replaced by a new pavilion. This was engineered by Mason Wood Architectural Consultants Ltd. who expanded the ideas of structural engineer, pier expert and NPS chairman David Bateman. The skating rink opposite the pier was opened in 2006. The re-furbished Winter Gardens pavilion includes a bar, restaurant, bowling alley, café, nightclub, amusements and shops. The designers missed a trick in not utilising the upper storey for views across Swansea Bay.

Part of the pier deck is under repair (author's collection)

CHRIS'S VERDICT: almost perfect
WALK TIME: 1 min 21 sec

First opened: 10 May 1898
Designer: W Sutcliffe Marsh (his only pier)
Contractor: Mayoh & Haley, Widnes Foundry
Construction: cast iron piles, lattice steelwork, pitch-pine deck
Original length: 835 ft (255 m)
Present length: 835 ft (255 m)
Restoration: 1950s, 1987/8
Legal: Mumbles Railway & Pier Acts 1889–1939
Original owners: Aberystwyth Pier Co.
Present owners: Bollom family
Website: www.mumbles-pier.co.uk

PAIGNTON

A homely and welcoming entrance (author's collection)

BRIGHT AND BREEZY

Instead of being hemmed in by the usual seaside clutter, Paignton Pier is approached across an open green sward. The pier entrance proper is in fact some way along the pier deck. The roof-line of the buildings along the pier neck is also unusual, but the ornate ballustrading and classic lamp standards are very much in keeping with the pier's Victorian design. A pleasing aspect of the main amusement arcade is that it has plenty of natural light. The pier itself is illuminated at night.

Local barrister Mr Arthur Hyde Dendy had a great idea. He actually bought Teignmouth Pier with the intention of transporting it, lock, stock and barrel, to Paignton. Fortunately, for both resorts, Mr Dendy found that was going to be too expensive. So instead he built a brand-new pier at Paignton. Plans were drawn up by the grandly-named architect George Soudon Bridgman, and the Paignton Pier Act received the Royal assent on 3 June 1874. Work started in 1878, and the pier opened in June 1879.

Two years later the pier head was enlarged and a Grand Pavilion and billiard-room ('with two fine billiard tables') added. The pavilion was elegantly decorated with brilliant lighting. It had a moveable stage, and among the orchestral instruments were a grand organ, grand piano, harmonium and kettledrums. At the pier entrance were cloakrooms, a refreshment room and a roller-skating rink. When Mr Dendy died, the pier was bought by the Devon Dock, Pier & Steamship Co.

The pier head and pavilion were destroyed by fire in June 1919. The firemen pulled timbers from the pier deck to stop the fire spreading along the pier.

Prior to 1939, the local council expressed interest in buying the pier but came up against local opposition. In 1940 the pier was sectioned but after World War II it was repaired. Alterations were made in 1968, and in 1980/1 the shoreward end was widened at a cost of £250,000. Mitchell Leisure took over in June 1994 and held a re-opening ceremony on 7 June 1995. This was to mark the first phase of restoration, which included work on the deck and the building of a new shore-end building.

The Gilbert and Sullivan operetta *The Pirates of Penzance* did not – as has often been said – have its premier on Paignton Pier, but it is a grand tale nonetheless. The fact is that, in order to protect the American copyright, *Pirates* had its official premier at the Fifth Avenue Theatre in New York on 31 December 1879. To secure the English copyright, a token single performance was given in England on the afternoon of 30 December. This did take place in Paignton, but at the Royal Bijou Theatre in the town and not on the pier.

The second *HMS Pinafore* company happened to be on tour that week and were in nearby Torquay. They gave the English premiere of *Pirates* at the Bijou in their *Pinafore* costumes, with handkerchiefs tied round their heads to denote piracy and with the scripts in their hands. Perhaps mercifully, it was a 'one off' performance. However, in July 1880, Mr D'Oyly Carte's full company did perform a Gilbert and Sullivan comic opera at the pier Pavilion, the piece re-titled for the occasion as *HMS Pinafore on the Water*. So there is more than a bit of truth in the story. And there is a (sort of) happy ending. D'Oyly Carte office manager, Helen Lenoir, who organised the English debut of *Pirates* at Paignton, married her boss – Richard D'Oyly Carte – in 1888. After his death in 1891, she took over running the company.

Paignton promenade and beach, c.1957
(Frances Foote collection)

Paignton Pier, 2007
(courtesy of Richard Stevens)

CHRIS'S VERDICT: a very distinctive pier
WALK TIME: 2 min 20 sec

Work started: 1878
First opened: 3 June 1879.
Designer: George Soudon Bridgman (his only pier)
Contractor: J Harris
Construction: cast iron screw piles in pairs with cross-bracing
Original length: 780 ft (238 m)
Present length: 740 ft (226 m)
Landing stage: yes
Fire: 1919
Restoration: 1881, 1948, 1968, 1980/1, 1994/5
Legal: Paignton Pier Act 1874
Present owners: UK Piers Ltd
Website: www.paigntonpier.co.uk

PAIGNTON

PENARTH

Broad pier deck with picnic tables (author's collection)

SUPERB ART DECO PAVILION

Penarth's main pavilion is another fine example of a building that is individual to its pier and helps define it visually. Built in 1929, it displays its art deco influence, described by some as 'festive' art deco. Four solid square three-storey towers with conical roofs sit firmly at each corner. The main body of the building is barrel-shaped, each side pierced by four windows of depth and character. A circular, colonnaded portico gives further character to the front of the building and defines a welcoming entrance into a small and friendly circular entrance hall – still with its original mouldings – in which the external columns are reflected. Unusually, the back of the pavilion is as good-looking as the front. Only the ground floor is in use at present, but this unique and well-balanced building will surely be refurbished soon.

Across the road is the former Public Baths, erected in 1884, which originally had seawater bathing. Now it is being converted into luxury apartments. Along the esplanade are the Italian Gardens which helped give Penarth its title of 'The Garden by the Sea'.

There is nothing garish about Penarth Pier. There are none of the usual seaside amusements. There are modern shops, cafes – one with tables outside on the pier approach – restaurants, a Tourist Information Centre, and a pub on the promenade. Water sports thrive here, with sailing, water-skiing and body-surfing all popular. Parking can be a problem at peak times, and driving along the esplanade is one-way.

There are a pair of mid-pier shelters housing a café and toilets, and a small building at the far end which serves the local fishing club and as a pay office for ferry passengers. Penarth Pier, always a popular landing-point for steamers, continues to provide a regular service for visitors who fancy a short sea cruise. The MV *Balmoral* and the *Waverley*, the world's last sea-going paddle steamer, are regular visitors. At the pier head there are seats but no telescopes.

The Penarth Promenade and Landing Pier Co. had considered buying the pier at Douglas, Isle of Man, but that went to Rhos-on-Sea on the North Wales coast, so they built their own. The pier, 658 feet long and 25 feet wide, opened on 4 February 1895. In 1907 a wooden Bijou Pavilion was built at the seaward end and later became a dance hall.

In June 1892 the *Penarth Observer* published a thundering editorial under the heading 'Pier Sham'. The *Observer* accused the Windsor family, whom owned most of Penarth, of misleading visitors and potential visitors to the resort town. The Penarth guide book, published by the Windsor Estates, showed a pier with a palatial reading room, a gym and bandstand – none of which it had. The pier had not even been built! The advert also claimed there were steamer excursions 'at all states of the tide', again not true. The Welsh Windsors, by the way, are not to be confused with the family of our own dear Queen, who changed their name from Saxe-Coburg to Windsor in 1917.

A concrete landing stage was added to Penarth Pier in 1927/8. The pier's striking shore-end art deco pavilion, still its main feature today, was built in 1929. On Monday, 3 August 1931, a fire broke out on the pier. There were 800 people in the Bijou Pavilion on the pier head, and a dramatic rescue ensued. All 800 escaped unharmed, but a large portion of the pier was damaged and the pavilion and some shelters and shops were destroyed. It cost £3,157 to repair the pier, but the pier-head pavilion was not replaced.

On 2 May 1947, the 7,131-ton vessel *Port Royal Park* was trying to gain entry to Cardiff Docks in a fierce gale. She was driven beyond the port entrance and into Penarth pier, causing damage which cost £28,000 to repair. The pier was closed for repairs, but eventually reopened in 1950. On 20 August 1966, the White Funnel paddler *Bristol Queen* hit Penarth Pier, again causing considerable damage. White Funnel cruises stopped in 1981. Much restoration has been done in recent years, £650,000-worth in 1994, £1.7 million in 1996, and £1.1 million in 1998 thanks to a Heritage Lottery Fund grant. Pier supporters helped by each paying £25 for a brass plaque on the pier deck.

Better still, a £2 million renovation scheme for Penarth Pier's superb shore-side art deco pavilion, is now up and running. The 1929 building fronting the pier, which still retains much of its original features, will be completely refurbished, subject to obtaining National Heritage Lottery funding. The pavilion, currently being used as a gym, will be the venue for plays, concerts, dances, art exhibitions and an annual film festival, if plans by Penarth Arts and Crafts Ltd. come to fruition.

Beach and pier, Penarth, c.1909 (courtesy of the National Piers Society)

Penarth Pier played a prominent role in the first official seamen's strike of 1911. In May of that year, J Havelock-Wilson, Lib-Lab MP and leader of the National Sailor's Union, sent *Captain* Edward Tupper to South Wales to organise the strike. This was in the years leading up to World War I, the German Kaiser was 'banging the drums of war' and there was much talk of anarchism, sedition and national security. In the subsequent court proceedings, F E Smith, later Lord Birkenhead, described Tupper as 'the most dangerous man in Europe'.

Tupper took up residence in Penarth, and the strike started on 14 June 1911. The shipowners responded through their Shipping Federation. To break the strike, the Federation anchored an old windjammer, the *Lady Jocelyn*, off the end of Penarth Pier. One afternoon, Tupper and a friend were walking along the pier and saw a crowd of Chinese 'blackleg' seamen come out of the Bijou Pavilion at the end of the pier and board a tug to be taken out to the *Lady J*. The tug belonged to Mr E Hancock of Penarth, a shipowner and not to be confused with Mr E Hancock of the Cardiff brewing family, a completely different bloke. This is Wales, remember, where more people than most share the same surname.

Tupper called out to Hancock, who was on the bridge of the tug, and remonstrated with him. According to Tupper, Hancock responded with 'filthy and unforgivable remarks'. Next day Tupper took himself to Hancock's offices in Bute Street, Cardiff, accompanied by a huge crowd of strikers. They surrounded the offices and Tupper challenged Hancock to fisticuffs 'anywhere he liked, in private or in public'. Hancock's answer was 'Go to Hell!' Someone then threw a lump of coal through one of the office windows, and someone else threw an open jack-knife.

The following day, Tupper was arrested on sixteen summonses. He made an appearance in court, one of many such, on 18 July 1911. Tupper was bailed for £800 – an enormous sum in those days. The case was heard in October that year. With the court packed with his supporters, the jury found Tupper not guilty on all sixteen counts. On another occasion, Tupper managed to get one of his men aboard the *Lady J* as cook. 'He carried aboard small stores which came from a chemist's shop,' says a contemporary report. The 'cook' doctored the grub on the *Lady J*, resulting in many blacklegs leaving the vessel. Eventually the remaining 'scabs' had to call for a doctor from the shore.

The *Lady Jocelyn* herself had a long and colourful career. Built in 1852, she was a three-masted, fully rigged iron ship, 2,242 gross tons, with an auxiliary engine. She made her maiden voyage from Plymouth to Calcutta in August 1852. In 1855 she transported troops to the Crimea, and in 1863 she took troops to New Zealand during the Second Maori War. Later the *Lady J* had her engines removed and made fourteen successive voyages as a sailing ship between the UK and New Zealand, the last in 1889 when she was bought by the Shipping Federation as a store ship in London's West India Docks. During World War I the *Lady J* was used as a floating barracks in the London docks. She was finally broken up in the Netherlands in 1922.

Penarth's art deco pavilion (author's collection)

Follies poster, 1930
(Phil Carradice collection)

Big waves on Penarth prom, 2007
(Phil Carradice collection)

Penarth: disembarking from the Penarth Ferry Kate (Phil Carradice collection)

The scheme to convert the pavilion into a fully-fledged arts centre was officially launched at the Senedd in Cardiff, home of the Welsh Assembly, in August 2007. Alun Michael MP, Councillor Margaret Alexander, leader of Vale of Glamorgan Council (owners of the building), Assembly Member Lorraine Barrett, and Penarth Mayor Gwyn Roberts, took part. There was not so much pomp and ceremony as in years past, but still confirmation of the continuing commitment by public bodies to our seaside piers. One aspect has most definitely changed, and very much for the better. In contrast to the male-dominated committees of the Victorian and Edwardian eras, two of the four main participants with executive authority were women – and the pavilion project is being led by a woman, Washington Gallery director, Maggie Knight.

At the other end of the pier, as it were, it was hoped that Penarth would be part of a planned high-speed link between South Wales, Minehead and Ilfracombe.

Penarth Pier, c.1907 (Frances Foote collection)

CHRIS'S VERDICT: fine pier, superb art deco pavilion
WALK TIME: 1 min 43 sec

Status: Grade II
Work started: 1894
First opened: 4 February 1895
Designer: H F Edwards (his only pier)
Contractor: J & A Mayoh
Construction: cast iron piles, steel cross-bracing, wooden deck, concrete landing stage
Original length: 658 ft (200 m)
Present length: 658 ft (200 m)
Ship collisions: 1947, 1966
Fire: 1931
Restoration: 1994, 1996–8, 2007/08
Legal: Penarth Promenade Pier Order 1924.
Original owners: Penarth Promenade and Landing Pier Co.
Present owners: Vale of Glamorgan District Council
Website: www.valeofglamorgan.gov.uk

RAMSEY QUEENS

Crowds & cars, c.1950 (courtesy of the Friends of Queens Pier)

A PIER WITH FEW EQUALS

A fine, fine pier, but sadly closed to the public. Still, it is a joy to behold from all vantage points – apart from the ghastly 1950s entrance building that looks like a toilet block, and an ugly one at that. This Victorian masterpiece – the pier I mean – has stood up to the rigours of the Irish Sea for over 120 years and deserves more than the present minimal maintenance.

The Isle of Man once had two pleasure piers. The one at Douglas was shipped off in 1895, lock, stock and barrel, to Rhos-on-Sea on the North Wales coast only to suffer eventual demolition. Ramsey Queens Pier still remains, guarded by 'dangerous structure – keep off' warning signs. The local Friends group is working hard to restore this very fine pier. Unable to have an event on the pier, Saturday, 30 June 2007 was 'Under the Pier Day'.

Ramsey Queens Pier was designed by Sir John Goode CE and built by Head Wrightson of Stockton. There was a pair of octagonal timber tollhouses at the pier entrance. A 500-feet landing platform was added in 1899. The pier, costing £45,000, was opened by Rowley Hill, the Bishop of Sodor and Man, on 22 July 1886. Queen Victoria gave her permission for it to be named the Queen's Pier. Several monarchs have landed at Ramsey Pier, including King George V and Queen Mary who landed here twice, on 14–15 July 1920.

The tramway along the pier was hauled manually until August 1899 when a small locomotive was introduced and passenger car added. For those driving their own cars, a small crane lifted them between the pier and steamship. In 1937 the 8 hp petrol locomotive *Planet* was brought into service on the pier. This was replaced in August 1950 by a new Whickham Railcar.

By 1906 36,000 passengers a year were using the pier, but after World War I numbers declined as most ships stopped at Douglas. In 1956 the attractive wooden Victorian kiosks at the pier entrance were replaced by the present drab building. Pier charges in 1963 were 4*d*. for adults and 2*d*. for children, one way. Passenger numbers dropped to 5,000 a year. The last steamer called in 1971, and the tramway ceased to operate in 1981. The 36-inch gauge tramway rails still seem to be in good order, but the two old bogies parked in the modest entrance hall are a forlorn sight. Neglect and vandalism finally forced the pier's closure in 1991.

The Friends of Ramsey Queens Pier, formed in 1994. They organised an annual walk on the pier which was stopped by the authorities in 2003 for health and safety reasons. The Friends responded by changing it into an 'Under the Pier' day. The Tynwald, the Manx parliament, has allocated £40,000 a year for maintenance but has so far been unable or unwilling to grasp the nettle and institute a full-scale refurbishment plan. As the Isle of Man is not formally part of the UK, or the EU for that matter, Lottery and other similar funding is not available.

Anti-vandal fencing – ugly but sadly necessary
(author's collection)

'Modern' front, not much cop to start with, now just plain ugly, complete face-lift needed
(author's collection)

The sign says it all
(author's collection)

Pier entrance, 1895 (courtesy of the Friends of Queens Pier)

CHRIS'S VERDICT: sadly closed, but well worth restoring
WALK TIME: n/a

Work started: 1882
First opened: 22 July 1886
Designer: Sir John Goode
Contractor: Head Wrightson & Co., Stockton
Construction: cast iron screw piles, circular iron columns braced by diagonal iron tie rods; longitudinal and transverse wrought iron lattice girders supporting transverse timbers and timber deck
Original length (i) 2244 ft (684 m); (ii) 2748 (838 m), 1897
Present length: 2244 ft (684 m)
Original owners: Isle of Man Harbour Board
Present owners: Isle of Man Government
Support group: Friends of Ramsey Queens Pier
Website: www.ramseypier.iofm.net

RYDE

Let the train take you to the pier head and the ferry (author's collection)

OUR OLDEST PIER – THREE-IN-ONE – AND THE RYDE ISLAND LINE IS A MIGHTY FINE LINE!

Dating from 1814, Ryde Pier on the Isle of Wight is the UK's oldest surviving seaside pier. It is actually three piers in one, and – even more remarkably – has London Underground trains running along it! The Ryde Island Line not only serves its busy ferry terminal and transports you up and down the pier, it also takes you along the Island's east coast. The Island Line is operated by former London Underground stock, brought to the Island in 1989 after 50 years' service on the Northern Line. And it actually does go underground for a spell, but not on the pier of course. Because it is a train, it has to have a driver and a guard. There is even the familiar 'Mind the Gap' painted on the platform edge. For 80 pence you can either ride or walk one way along the pier.

The Island Line is eight miles long. It goes from Ryde pier head to the landside station, then on to Smallbrook Junction, Brading, Sandown, Lake and Shanklin. Owned by Stagecoach and part of the South West Trains franchise, it operates 29 times a day and is 99.7% punctual. There are two rail lines on the pier, but only one is now in use.

Ryde Pier is unusual, if not unique, in being built as 'three piers in one', adjacent but separate. As you look from the shore, to the left is the original pier, built for pedestrians and now adapted for cars. It was the first major passenger piled pier. Now walkers are relegated to a narrow strip of tarmac, separated from the traffic only by a line of paint – not very conducive to comfort and safety, let alone peace of mind. This pier still carries two small Victorian shelters from which the seats have been removed. Running between the two other piers is the long-abandoned Tramway Pier, opened on 29 August 1864. Its rusting iron and steelwork is a highly visible and an ugly reminder of what neglect will do in the unforgiving environment of the seashore. Then on the right is the Ryde Train Pier with its solid concrete foundations, opened on 12 July 1880. There is a walkway on the far side, accessible from the pier-head station.

The pier-head rail station has a café, bar and a roomy waiting room. This pavilion has twin towers, impressive from a distance, that make it look like a mini-Wembley (old style). There is plenty of car-parking at the end of the pier, but no seats, but there is fishing at £3 a day, £1.50 for children and pensioners. So anglers are catered for, but walkers and strollers seem to be somewhat discouraged by the traffic and lack of seating at the pier head. The side of the pier-head station building is large, plain and ugly – plain ugly in fact. It is crying out for an eye-catching mural. Transporting people to and from the ferries remains Ryde Pier's main *raison d'etre*.

Close to the pier entrance is the bus station – very convenient – and a café with good views of the pier. Across the road, I bought a pier postcard for a mere 10 pence, just missing out on the cheapest cards in the British Isles. There are plans for a new transport interchange at the pier entrance, linking trains, buses and the Southsea hovercraft which operates from close by.

The origins of Ryde Pier go back much further than 1814. In 1420 the Lord of the Manor of Ashey claimed the right to control boats carrying passengers between 'Ride' and Portsmouth. Following an Act of Parliament in 1812, the first Ryde Pier of the three we can see today, was built and opened on 26 July 1814. It was 1,740 feet long, in 33 bays with a flight of steps at the end. A gale in March 1818 damaged 750 feet of the pier, but it was repaired and, in 1824, extended by a further 300 feet. A landing stage was also added. In 1833 the pier was extended once again to 2,250 feet and equipped with an 'octogan lamp' for navigation. Despite this, a brig crashed into the pier in an 1838 gale and took out 50 feet of the deck. In 1842 the first pier head was built to take Ryde Pier to its present length of 2,305 feet (703 metres) long. In 1851–3, the pier was widened to 20 feet, and in 1860 a second, diamond-shaped pier head was built. From 1895–1911, the wooden piles were replaced by iron. In the 1930s the pier head was rebuilt in concrete.

Under the 1812 Act, pier tolls for passengers was 3*d*.; for walkers, 2*d*.; riders on horseback, 4*d*.; four-wheeled carriages, 1*s*.; and for two-wheeled carriages, 6*d*. Landing a horse attracted a 9*d*. charge; a bull, cow or ox, 6*d*.; a hog or pig, 2*d*. Sheep were 1*s*. 2*d*. for 20, or a penny a head for fewer than 20. Lambs were 1*s*. for 20, calves 2*d*. each, four-wheeled carts, 3*s*.; and two-wheeled carts 2*s*. Porters paid £30 a year (which was increased to £45 in November 1842) for the privilege of plying for business on the pier, making their money from charges and tips. The Pier Co. employed a sweeper to clean up after sheep and other livestock that had traversed the pier. In 1856 a certain Mr W H Smith (now where have I seen that name?) built a bookstall on the pier.

Ryde Pier's 'twin towers' (author's collection)

As first built, the timber decking of Ryde Pier was unsuitable for horse-drawn carriages, so the only way to get to the pier head was to walk. This was a long trek and very unpleasant in bad weather. So a second pier, the Ryde Tramway Pier, was built alongside the original pier and opened on 29 August 1864. The trams went from the pier head to the esplanade, and on to Ryde itself – even going

The Queen Elizabeth *passes Ryde Pier, c.1950 (Frances Foote collection)*

Ryde Pier, c.1909. Today cars drive along the promenade deck (Frances Foote collection)

Ryde pier head: arrival of a steamer, c.1906 (courtesy of the National Piers Society)

through the middle of Holywell House. The trams were horse-drawn until 1885, when the line was electrified. This was one of the first electric railways in the world, even earlier than the London Underground.

In 1927 petrol-engine trams were introduced on the tram pier, converted to diesels in 1959. The pier trams remained in service until 1969. Since then the Tramway Pier has basically been left to rot. You can see its sad, rusting skeleton between Ryde Pier and the newest of the *troika*, the Railway Pier. This was first set in motion (excuse the pun) in 1878 when plans were drawn up by the London and South Western, and the London, Brighton and South Railway Companies to connect Ryde's pier head and Ryde's St John's Road stations via a rail pier and a tunnel, at a cost of £250,000. The St John's Road station, on the line to Shanklin, had been opened in August 1864 and was the island's first rail station. The Railway Pier, half a mile long and connecting to the existing pier head, opened in July 1880. The Southern Railway took over the pier in 1924. In 1966/7, the route was electrified and old London Underground stock brought in. If you board the train at the pier head, you can travel as far south as Shanklin.

On 18 January 1881, the collier *Havelock* smashed into Ryde Pier. Three days later, on 21 January, another coal-carrying ship, the *John Warder* also hit the pier. Over 300 feet of deck had to be replaced. In 1887 people petitioned for a pavilion at Ryde Pier Head, a place where they could enjoy music and other entertainment. The resultant fine, octagonal, domed two-storey building – containing reading and refreshments rooms, a concert hall and an upstairs sun lounge – hosted such luminaries as 1960s groups *Amen Corner* and *Dave Dee, Dozey, Beaky Mick & Tich*. For some years the pavilion was managed by the father of author and biographer Hunter Davies.

CHRIS'S VERDICT: fascinating pier train, but no viewing seats
WALK TIME: 7 min 01 sec

Status: Grade II
Work started: 29 July 1813
First opened: 26 July 1814
Designer: John Kent (his only pier)
Construction: originally wood, replaced by iron; pier head supports in concrete
Original length: (i) 1740 ft (531 m); (ii) 2040 ft (622 m), 1824; (iii) 2250 ft (686 m), 1842
Present length: 2305 ft (703 m)
Ship collisions: 1881, 2003
Restoration: 1896, 1947, 1960s, 1970/1, 1982, 1987/8
Legal: Ryde Pier Act 1812
Original owners: Ryde Pier Co.
Present owners: Wight Line Ferries Ltd.
Pier of the Year: 1999
Website: www.island-line.co.uk

ST ANNES

The Pier Pavilion, St. Annes-on-the-Sea

St Annes Pier Pavilion, c.1904 (courtesy of St Annes Pier Co.)

WHERE GRACIE FIELDS PERFORMED

A mock-Tudor entrance, built around 1900, gives St Annes Pier its unique atmosphere. Between the more popular north-west resorts of Southport and Blackpool, St Annes still holds its own with the pier its anchor. Here on the sand – and not on the pier – Gracie Fields made her seaside debut in 1903 as a fifteen-year-old Pierrot before returning to star at the pier theatre. Young Gracie, already a seasoned trouper, was the lead girl soprano in the show at *Freddie Carlton's Cosy Corner*, performed at an improvised open-air 'pavilion' created by simply putting up windbreaks among the sand dunes. She got £3 a week – not bad for a fifteen-year-old.

As well as 'our Gracie', George Formby, Bob Monkhouse and Russ Conway played at the Floral Hall, which had opened in 1910. Conway recalls he got the princely sum of £75 a week as top of the bill in 1958. Cliff Richard also made an appearance. A 1965 charity concert had Freddie Frinton and Jewel & Warris at the top of the bill, and a young Mike Yarwood well down the order.

The children's theatre half-way along the pier was damaged by fire in 1959, but the following year the pier got a new deck and a restaurant. In 1962 the pier was bought for £240,000 by the Amalgamated Investment & Property Co. It was renovated in the style of a luxury liner, with 500 deckchairs. Improvements were made to the pavilion, Floral Hall, landing jetty and children's section. In 1966 the Floral Hall was converted into a Tyrolean Beer Garden. In 1970 the Moorish Pavilion became the Sultan's Palace, featuring belly-dancers, fire-eater and snake charmers. That year 250,000 adults and 100,000 children paid the pier admission.

7 June 1974 saw HRH Princess Anne attend a charity concert, but shortly afterwards the Sultan's Palace was destroyed in a fire and the new owners went into liquidation. Following a 6,000-signature petition to save it, the pier was sold and restoration work began, only for another

fire to destroy the Floral Hall on 22 July 1982. The length of the pier was reduced by 120 feet, but the pier was again refurbished in the early 1990s.

The 945 feet pier was built for the St Anne's-on-the-Sea Land & Building Company Ltd. at a cost of £18,000. It was opened on 15 June 1885 by Lord Derby (Colonel Fred Stanley MP). It had Chinese-style kiosks and elegant ironwork, and much of the latter is still in evidence. The landing stage was recon-structed in 1891. The famous 1,000-seat 'fairy tale' Moorish Pavilion was opened on 2 April 1904, as well as an extension to the pier, constructed at a cost of £30,000. The Floral Hall was built in 1910. The amusement arcade at the entrance was built in 1954 at a cost of £8,000.

Much shorter than it was, half the remaining St Annes Pier is taken up by its extensive amusement arcade. Outside, the main pavilion looks fine with its rows of minarets. The pier neck looked inviting but was closed for repairs on my visit. It was re-opened soon afterwards. It has two handsome shelters and there are plenty of seats on either side. The supporting steelwork looks delicate, as befits an estuary pier.

Close to the pier stands the imposing monument to Coxwain William Johnson and the crew of the St Annes' lifeboat who all perished in a gallant attempt to rescue the crew of the German barque *Mexico*, wrecked off Southport on the night of 9 December 1886.

St Annes' unique half-timbered 'Tudor Mansion' pier front will remain after renovation. And, it is 4.30, surely time for tea?
(author's collection)

Aerial view, c.1965 (courtesy of St Annes Pier Co.)

St Annes, c.1955. 'Princess' pram – with baby aboard – front left (Frances Foote collection)

Paddling at St Annes, c.1910 (Richard Riding collection)

A regatta on 9 September 1899 attracted 1,594 paying customers on the pier. It was 2*d*. for strollers, and 1*d*. for passengers embarking on a sea trip. Clog dancing was still being performed on St Annes Pier in 1965. The same year, comedian Les Dawson found himself brought in as a last-minute substitute for Irish tenor Joseph Locke who had failed to turn up.

'An almost perfect example of Victorian pier design' – government report.

CHRIS'S VERDICT: small but (almost) perfectly formed
WALK TIME: 1 min 17 sec (pavilion only)

First opened: 15 June 1885
Designer: Alfred Dowson
Construction: iron columns, iron lattice girders
Original length: 914 ft (279 m)
Present length: 600 ft (183 m)
Fire: 1959, 1974, 1982
Restoration: 1904, 1954, 1960, 1962, 1990s
Legal: St. Annes-on-the-Sea Pier Orders 1879–1923
Original owners: St Anne's-on-the-Sea Land & Building Co.
Present owners: Clark Leisure Catering
Website: www.visitlancashire.com

SALTBURN

Surfing safari (author's collection)

YORKSHIRE'S ONLY REMAINING SEASIDE PIER

England's most northerly pier is at Saltburn. Taking the short walk from the station, or parking your car on Marine Parade at the top of the cliff, you could be asking: 'where's the pier?' Now much shorter that it used to be – like so many of our seaside piers – Saltburn's seaside gem only comes into view when you reach the sign directing you 'to the pier.'

And what a gem it is! A straight and simple structure, still defying the North Sea after nearly 140 years. The shore-side building with its distinctive triple roof is brightly decorated in red and white, but there is nothing garish about Saltburn's pier. There are amusements, of course, but they are small-scale and friendly. There is a tearoom, walks along the lower promenade and the pier itself, plus excellent sandy beaches. And before that, to get down to the pier from the top of the cliff, Saltburn's iconic funicular railway, surely one of our most scenic pier lifts.

Before you enjoy your railway ride, just take in the view. The North Sea, so often deceptively calm, can throw up waves good enough for surfers to make Saltburn a regular base. To your right are the brooding cliffs of Saltburn Scar, atop of which runs the Cleveland Way footpath. Beneath the cliffs you see the Ship Inn and a row of cottages that surely provided a haven for smugglers. In fact, this is where you will find the Saltburn Smugglers Heritage Centre!

Before the Stockton and Darlington railway was extended to Saltburn in 1861, the village was described as: 'a small sixteen-house hamlet situated upon the sea and under a mountain, with quaint villagers engaged in fishing and seal catching, but mainly smuggling.' The railway, the magnificent Zetland Hotel, the Ha'Penny Bridge (now demolished) and the pier turned Saltburn into a famous Victorian seaside resort.

Even if you are a fitness fanatic who loves nothing better than walking up and down steep slopes at every opportunity, do go on the cliff lift. It is a smooth and comfortable ride, and retains all

It is five past ten and you can get a 'lift to town'
(author's collection)

This old brake-wheel did duty – without a single failure –
for 128 years! (author's collection)

the charm of its Victorian construction and design. Saltburn Pier was designed and built by local man John Anderson. Contrary to some reports, Sir John Goode and Head Wrightson had nothing to do with it. Anderson had been an engineer on the Stockton–Darlington Railway. He built the Alexandra Hotel on Saltburn seafront. He formed the Saltburn-by-the-Sea Pier Company in October 1867 and was both designer and contractor for the project. The ironwork was provided by the Ormesby Foundry Company. The first pile was driven on 27 January 1868, and the pier was opened in May 1869, the first in Cleveland. It was a great success, attracting over 50,000 visitors in the first month.

Saltburn Pier was originally 1,500 feet long with a steamer landing stage at the seaward end. There were services linking Bridlington, Scarborough and Hartlepool. There was even a small theatre, added later. Huge storms in 1874 and 1875 destroyed the landing stage and part of the main structure, but the pier was repaired and re-opened in 1877 with refreshment rooms. A new pier head was built, although the pier was reduced in length to 1,250 feet. The pier owners had the good sense also to install windshields! A bandstand was added in 1885.

The pier lost another 120 feet and the pier head was damaged in a storm in early 1900. In May 1924 the ship *Ovenbeg* – which had a name change to the *St Nicolai* – crashed into the pier, leaving a 210-foot gap. With visitors obviously unable to get to the bandstand, a small theatre was built at the landward end. By 1930 the pier was back in business.

The local council bought Saltburn Pier in 1938, but the onset of World War II the following year brought the danger of a German invasion. Like so many piers on our south and east coats, Saltburn's had a section cut out by the Royal Engineers to prevent German troops using it as a handy landing-spot. Repairs got underway in 1947, and after repairs costing £20,000 the pier finally re-opened in April 1952.

Just one year later, another North Sea storm took a terrible toll on the whole structure, twisting it out of shape. Rebuilding work was not completed until 1958. There was yet more storm damage in 1959, and again in 1961 when 20 piles had to be repaired. In 1967 it was decided that only the outermost 13 trestles needed to be taken out. After more storm damage in 1971 and 1973, the pier was closed on safety grounds. Another storm on 29 October 1974 destroyed the pier head and damaged the rest of the pier, and Saltburn Pier was on the way out!

In 1975 the council applied for listed building consent to demolish the pier, only to provoke a 'Save Our Pier' campaign. After a public inquiry the following year, a rescue plan was agreed. This allowed for the 17 end trestles to be removed and the remainder of the pier to be restored. The whole job cost £71,000. Now reduced to 681 feet, Saltburn Pier re-opened in June 1978. In 1993 the roof of the landward building was renewed with Welsh and Westmorland slate, but by 1996 Saltburn Pier was again in imminent danger of collapse.

Finally, in 2000, the millennium year brought a £1.2 million Heritage Lottery Fund grant which funded the repair of the cast iron trestles and new wooden decking replacing steel to restore the deck's original appearance. Finance was also provided by the European Regional Development Fund, Redcar and Cleveland Borough Council, Saltburn Improvement Co., One North East, and

En passent (author's collection)

Shall we walk down or ride down? Every 'down' passenger reduces the electricity bill. It is true, I tell you!
(author's collection)

the Friends of Saltburn Pier, among others. After yet another official opening in 2001, we now see Saltburn Pier restored to something like its former glory. It is as fresh and bright as it was in 1869, if only half its original length.

The original structure consisted of wrought iron piles driven into the seabed, supporting cast iron trestles with cross-bracing, topped by timber beams under the wooden deck. In restoring the pier, it was found necessary to anchor the original piles deeper into the shale rock strata that underlies the sand. Steel beams were replaced by timber, as in the original construction, giving a more flexible structure.

Re-opened on 13 July 2001 by Chris Smith MP, former Secretary of State for Culture, Media and Sport. In 2002 Saltburn Pier won the first Peter Mason Award for restoration or new pier building work, done in this case by Robert Stone Associates of Norwich. Mason is a former president of the Institute of Structural Engineers and chairman of the National Piers Society. On 6 October 2005, new pier lighting was switched on, courtesy of the provision of £385,000 by Redcar Borough Council. The lighting system installed in 2005 has given the pier at night the appearance of being bathed in moonlight, even when there is no moon.

The restoration has a pleasing simplicity about it, but there is also a practical purpose. It has been designed for minimal maintenance. Only the railings and the pier deck will require regular attention. Otherwise, it is claimed, Saltburn Pier will be good for another 140 years. The plain, three-bar rails have been fitted with a substantial toe board along the bottom – an excellent innovation which hopefully will stop small objects, small animals and small children falling off the deck.

Saltburn beach and pier, c.1903 (courtesy of the National Piers Society)

The deck is built with strong, substantial planking, fixed by countersunk bolts, comfortable to walk on and reassuringly strong.

This is a plain pier, but one with lots of character. The deck has a slight upward slope for the first third, then levels off before reaching its small, square head. There are a few seats. There would be more, but the council has put an embargo on any more seats being placed until an outstanding court case is resolved. It seems that someone is suing the council for damages after walking into one of the seats at night. My one criticism is that there are only two litter bins on the pier, albeit discreet ones. My guess is that the litter on the pier deck results from overflowing bins.

In 2006 Saltburn Pier was voted runner-up to Worthing in the National Piers Society's annual Pier of the Year awards and in 2007 Saltburn came third. In the nineteenth century, the North Sea was known as the German Ocean. When a new bridge was built on the foreshore just along from the pier, the old bridge was found to have graffiti from World War II – a message in German 'welcoming' Hitler's troops in the event of invasion.

Vertical cliff lift, c.1880 (Tony Flynn collection)

CHRIS'S VERDICT: one of the best pier restorations I have ever seen
WALK TIME: 2 min 11 sec

Status: Grade II*
Work started: 27 January 1868
First opened: May 1869
Designer: John Anderson (his only pier)
Contractor: John Anderson
Construction: cast iron trestles under a wooden deck
Original length: 1500 ft (458 m)
Present length: 681 ft (206 m)
Storm damage: 1874, 1875, 1900, 1953, 1961, 1971, 1973, 1974
Ship collision: May 1924
Restoration: 1877, 1930, 1952, 1978, 2000
Legal: Saltburn and Marske-by-Sea UDC Act 1938
Original owners: Saltburn-by-the-Sea Pier Co.
Present owners: Redcar and Cleveland Borough Council
Support group: Friends of Saltburn Pier and Cliff Lift
Pier of the Year: 2006 (runner-up)
Websites: www.marskebythesea.co.uk, www.visitsaltburn.co.uk

SANDOWN CULVER

Morning sun (author's collection)

'A WHOLE DAY'S FUN IN ONE'

As piers go, Sandown is somewhat plain. But if you are having fun – and there is any amount of fun to be had – then who is worried about the architecture? Sandown boasts a genuine helter-skelter (now named a 'snake slide') at the pier head, as well as all the other seaside attractions you would expect on a pier devoted to entertainment, fun and sheer enjoyment.

There is free admission to the pier, although the only entrance is through the extensive landside amusement arcade. There are two sidewalks, but these are closed to the public. One restriction is 'no hats or hoodies'. Through the arcade and onto the pier neck, the deck slopes down a few feet. You then pass through a mini-fair with booths on both sides to get to the pier head, which is also devoted to fun, apart from a concrete extension for anglers that forms a hollow square at a lower level. For the fishing cognoscenti, pendulum- and side-casting are not allowed.

The views here are not so dramatic, but there are seats and tables under cover. The shore end has a casino, an ice-cream parlour. The pier head has crazy golf, tenpin bowling, dodgems, children's adventure play area, and rides. On shore, you can hire deckchairs, sunbeds, windbreaks and 'surf canoes', all at your own risk. There is parking along the esplanade. The pier stands on pairs of rakes piles with cross-bracing. A composite beam runs along each side of the deck. Steel and concrete piles support the land-end pavilion.

A 360 feet pier under the Culver Cliff was started in 1876 but only partly completed by 1879. After failing to raise funds to improve and extend the pier, the original company failed and the pier was put up for auction. A new company – the Sandown Pier Extension Co. Ltd. - took over, and the pier was extended to 875 feet and a pier-head pavilion seating 400 and costing £12,000 was built. Paddle steamers could now call at the new landing stage. The 'new pier' opened on

Tuesday, 17 September 1895. The new pier and pavilion was opened by Miss Webster, sister of the Attorney-General, Sir Richard Everard Webster GCMG QC, who was also Viscount Alverstone and the newly-elected MP for the Isle of Wight. On the following Saturday, the local newspaper the *Isle of Wight County Press* gave the event the full treatment:

> The gaiety of Sandown on Tuesday was of a phenomenal character and has never been eclipsed in the history of this popular and rising watering-place. Everything combined to add to the success of the day's proceedings – the intense popularity of the Attorney-General in the town, the pleasure of its people at the metamorphosis of what was truly termed a ghastly skeleton into a thing of beauty and enjoyment, and the arrival of the epoch in the life of the town which this metamorphosis marked; lastly, the summer-like weather which bathed the beautiful bay and the bunting-bedecked front with brilliant sunshine. The proceedings began with a luncheon at the Royal Pier Hotel at which representatives of nearly all the public bodies in the Island were present.

The guests included the mayors of Newport and Ryde; the chairmen of Sandown, East Cowes; Ventnor and East Cowes district councils and Sandown Rural District Council; the Lord of the Manor; the vicar of Sandown; the vicar of St John's, Sandown; the Congregational, Baptist and Bible Christian ministers; Major Hopkins, of the local Artillery; Captain Arnell, of the Sandown Volunteers; Major Brown, of the Town Band; Captain Dore of the Sandown Fire Brigade; Major Seeley MP; representatives of the Dandy Dinmont Shipping Co.; contractors Grace and Roe; Mr James Colenutt, chairman of the pier company; Mr W H Wooldridge, company secretary; Messrs W E Green, F Dabell, C F Fox, Viney, F Duff (pier company directors); Dr Davey JP, chairman of the Ryde Pier directors; and Mr H Roberts, secretary and manager of the Ryde Pier Co. 'The lunch itself reflected the highest credit on the cuisine of the hotel and upon all concerned', said the newspaper.

After loyally honouring 'The Queen', the Mayor of Newport, Alderman Francis Pittis JP, proposed the toast 'Success to Sandown Pier'. He said:

> [he] could remember that not many years ago when Sandown was not the rising watering-place it is at the present time, from Wilke's Cottage down to the old fort there was scarcely a house; now that part was covered with residences filled with visitors during the season. A few years ago some of their enterprising inhabitants started a project for a Pier, without which a seaside resort of that kind would not be complete. That Pier had now, owing he understood to the energy of fresh directors, been lengthened to nearly 900 feet, and a noble pavilion, which they would presently see, had been erected at the end of it, capable of seating about 400 people, the total cost being about £12,000.

> That would show them what the spirit of the Sandown people, backed up as it had been by friends, would endeavour to do for the benefit of the town and the Island generally [applause]. In addition, to have a spacious landing-place at which steamers could embark passengers for the various parts of the Isle of Wight must be of considerable advantage to the town and trade of Sandown [applause]. He understood that, thanks to the energy and attention paid to the works by the eminent contractors who had them in hand only about ten months – during a great part of which time stormy weather had prevailed, since they commenced operations [applause] – now, in the middle of the season, they had the Pier opened for visitors, and he thought they would all agree that it was a most spacious one, well built and well founded in every respect [applause].

Success to Sandown or any other part of the Island meant success to the whole Isle of Wight [*hear, hear*, applause]. If one town prospered the others did so in proportion. He saw the motto had been prepared for illumination 'Forward Sandown,' and he thought he could adopt no better one than in giving them this toast [applause]. He wished the Board, the Town, and the whole Isle of Wight success [applause].

James Colenutt, chairman of the Sandown Pier Extension Co., replied in like fashion. He referred to the establishment of the Isle of Wight Waterworks Co. and the Junction Railway to Newport. The previous pier company 'had considerable difficulty in raising sufficient capital, owing to the fears of some that it would not pay, and the opposition of others, who said it would spoil the place and was not needed'. It went into liquidation, 'leaving the half Pier more of an excrescence that otherwise, a mere elevated stage over the sands, neither useful nor ornamental, eliciting remarks which were not very complimentary … Sandown might now be said to be complete, and ought to be, as it was, a place of great attraction [*hear, hear*, applause] … by availing themselves of the pleasure, the enjoyment, and convenience afforded by the Pier the public would contribute towards the fulfilment of the sentiment contained in the toast, and crown the undertaking with success [applause]'.

The Mayor of Ryde toasted to the health of the engineer and contractor. Saunders and Grace replied. Pier director Mr Fox gave the last toast. He joked that, as the pier and Sir Richard's son and heir Arthur Webster, were about the same age, they must have been 'thought of' about the same time [laughter and applause]. He hoped that Mr Arthur would have the same iron constitution as the pier. In his reply, Sir Richard admitted that he had not been in favour of a pier at Sandown, but 'to have a half-finished pier standing out like a ghastly skeleton on the sands was prejudicial to the prosperity of any place and that the only thing to do was to complete it'. Piers where steamboats could land were crucial to attracting visitors to the Island.

The assembled company then proceeded to the pier where Miss Webster was presented with a 'shower bouquet' and the key to the gates. The combined town bands of Sandown, Shanklin and Ventnor 'played most splendidly' in front of the pavilion, which 'was beautified by a number of handsome palms and ferns, coleus, and other plants'. After his sister had declared the new pier open, Sir Richard said he was sure the pier and pavilion would 'prove a lasting source of enjoyment, recreation and amusement to residents and visitors', which raised further applause. Afterwards, he entertained 'a large company' to tea.

Sandown Pier on fire, August Bank Holiday, 1989 (courtesy of Sandown Fire Station)

Fire damage (courtesy of Sandown Fire Station)

During the afternoon there were a series of aquatic sports: sailing matches, single and double sculls, water polo, canoe and galley races, and a 'shoving match' for watermen. The first three in the ladies' single sculls were sisters: Miss M Withers, Miss E Withers and Miss Ethel Withers winning cash prizes of 15*s.*, 10*s.* and 5*s.* respectively. In the evening there was entertainment: songs, harp solos and a whistling sketch. Finally, there were the illuminations. 'The Pier was illuminated with gas stars, lanterns and Vauxhall lamps at night. Many of the houses were prettily treated, the Battery House being especially well done. There was also a display of fireworks. Some 4,300 persons were on the pier'.

The above is only part of a much longer report. The speeches would have been recorded in shorthand notes and then hand-written or typed up. The text would then be set in hot metal type before being printed and delivered to readers avid to take in every detail of a major event in the town.

In 1897 bathing was allowed from the pier head, 6 a.m. to 1 p.m. weekdays, but 8–10 a.m. only on Sundays. 'Full bathing costume must be worn after 10 a.m.' warned the notices. Bathing machines that were wheeled into the sea were used up until 1918 when changing cubicles were provided. The sea wall and esplanade were constructed in about 1889.

Lord Alverstone died in 1915. In 1918 Sandown Urban District Council bought the pier from his estate for £2,500. The council reduced the pier toll from 'tuppence' to a penny and sold annual tickets for five shillings. In January 1919 the pier master's wages were increased from 25*s.* to 30*s.* a week. Admission to the Sunday concerts was 6*d.* for the plush seats and 3*d.* for wooden seats. In the 1930s a day excursion to Cherbourg by the paddle steamer *Balmoral* was 12*s.* 6*d.*. Boat trips from the pier ceased on 13 September 1967.

A new 980-seat pavilion costing £26,000 was opened on 23 October 1934 by Admiral of the Fleet, Earl Jellicoe. As befits a sailor, the Earl made a 'breezy speech'. 'It was a wonderful achievement to have erected the pavilion in five months,' he said. All the material used was empire material, 60% of the men employed were Island men, and all the cement, timber and bricks came from Island depots. But the Earl did complain: 'When one goes about in a motor-car in the summer, one is always being held up by charabancs.'

The pier was sectioned during the war, but was repaired and re-opened in 1947. A new double-decker landing stage was opened in 1954. The council rebuilt the pier from 1968 onwards. A new bar and café complex costing £392,000 was built, replacing the old fire-damaged pavilion. Earl Mountbatten, governor of the Isle of Wight and Admiral of the Fleet, carried out the official re-opening ceremony on 22 July 1973.He joked that Sandown Pier had been 'nationalised' when the council bought it in 1918. Mountbatten had served under a predecessor of his, Earl Jellicoe, who had opened the pier concert hall in 1934. On another occasion, Earl Mountbatten and the mayor, Councillor Desmond Price, accompanied the Queen when she strolled along Sandown Pier.

In 1986 Sandown Pier Ltd. under George Peak bought the pier. He spent nearly £500,000 on refurbishing it. In 1987 nearby Shanklin Pier was completely destroyed in a huge storm. Wreckage was strewn along the beach as far as Sandown, and local children had a great time digging in the sand for pots of money from the fruit machines! The remains of the pier were blown up.

Sandown Chronicle Page 20

Did You Know That

Did you know that on the 15th July 1965. Queen Elizabeth 11 appointed the Earl of Mountbatten as Governor of the Isle of Wight within a vibrant and colourful pageantry at Carisbrooke Castle.

The photograph presents Her Majesty the Queen at Sandown in the Company of Councillor Desmond Price with Lord Louis Mountbatten trailing in the rear.

Lord Mountbatten tragically lost his life in September 1979.

T. Hall (Sandown Archive)

The Queen on Sandown Pier
(Baldock family collection)

Sandown Pier, c.1915
(Baldock family collection)

On August Bank Holiday 1989, Sandown Pier itself was engulfed by a huge fire, causing £2 million-worth of damage. The fire started in an electrical switch box in the amusement arcade. Comedian Jimmy Tarbuck was appearing at the pier theatre, and he swore he would be back on stage at the first opportunity. Pier manager Terry Derrick had the same idea: 'You just don't roll over and die, do you?' he said. Seventy firemen and ten fire engines fought the blaze, which destroyed 50 amusement machines and much else besides, including three doves left in the dressing-room by illusionist Richard de Vere. It took four hours to bring the blaze under control.

The shoreward end of the pier re-opened within 30 hours of the blaze, and the pier was fully back in business with a 'grand re-opening' on Monday, 18 June 1990. The refurbishment involved eight miles of electrical cabling, three and a half miles of scaffolding, three miles of deck planking, 2,400 square metres of carpet, 980 theatre seats, 85 theatre lanterns, 900 sheets of plasterboard, a ton of nails and 20,000 screws!

Sandown Culver Pier, c.1935 (Frances Foote collection)

In the evening there was a 'spectacular fireworks extravaganza, lazers [*sic*] and light show – the Island's biggest event!' Not a modest man, Mr George Peak. The display caused a flood of 999 emergency phone calls to the Island police switchboard at Newport, reporting 'strange lights' in the sky. Callers were reassured that it was not a fire, nor was it UFOs paying a visit. The pier theatre, which had featured stars like Diana Dors, Petula Clark, Roy Castle, Dick Emery, Jim Davison, Cilla Black, Lenny Henry and Cannon & Ball, closed for good in 1997. Stars like Julie Andrews, Des O'Connor and Tony Hancock were all said to have started their careers on Sandown Pier which also featured impressionist Janet Brown, Bernie Clifton (plus ostrich), Bill and Marion Pertwee, and Norman Collier. The theatre area was turned into a mini-crazy golf course, a tenpin bowling and Magic Island play area.

CHRIS'S VERDICT: does what it says, a whole day's fun
WALK TIME: 2 min 45 sec

Work started: (i) 1876
First opened: (i) 1879; (ii) 17 September 1895
Designer: (i) W Binns; (ii) Theodore Saunders
Contractor: (i) Jukes and Coulson; (ii) Roe and Grace
Construction: pairs of cast iron piles with cross bracing, iron girder framework supporting timber deck
Original length: (i) 360 ft (110 m); (ii) 875 ft (297 m), 1895
Present length: 875 ft (297 m)
Ship collisions: 2003
Fire: 1989
Restoration: 1895, 1934, 1954, 1968, 1971–3, 1986
Legal: Sandown Pier Act 1864
Original owners: Sandown Pier Extension Co.
Present owners: Sandown Pier Leisure Ltd.
Pier of the Year: 1999
Websites: www.sandown-pier.com, www.wightindex.com

SKEGNESS

Skegness Pier, c.1950 *(Tim Mickleburgh collection)*

'ALL THE FUN OF THE PIER'

You can enter Skegness Pier from every direction: through the large amusement arcade or the bowling centre, or from the beach on either side, or by steps on the north side of the pier. On the pier deck behind the arcade there is a mini-fair, but the remainder of the pier is free for promenaders to enjoy, including a few seats. The delicate tracery of the railings and the old-style lamp standards – recently installed – give Skegness Pier a real period feel. There are telescopes and something new to observe – a wind farm under construction way out on the horizon. Judging by the size of the bases, the wind turbines themselves will be absolutely huge.

Landowner, the Earl of Scarborough, was instrumental in bringing the railway to 'Skeggy' and it was the Earl who formed the Skegness Pier Company in 1877. Getting his railway to bring holiday-makers to go on his pier was excellent Victorian business enterprise! There was a competition to design the pier, and Clarke & Pickwell's winning design was chosen from 44 entries. Each entrant got a £50 premium for their trouble. Work began in 1880, it cost £20,840, and the 1,817-foot pier was opened on 4 June 1881 by the Duke of Edinburgh. The T-shaped pier head carried a 700-seat concert hall and a landing stage where steamers docked from 1882. In 1898 the pier-head saloon was extended and new refreshment rooms built.

However, in March 1919 the schooner *Europa* breached the pier. A temporary gangway was put across the resultant gap by August of that year, but full restoration was not completed until 1939 when a café and shops were added to the entrances built in 1929/30.

In 1932, after a notorious court case, Harold Davidson, the Rector of Stiffkey in Norfolk, was convicted of immoral behaviour and de-frocked by the Church of England. Davidson then joined the circus and spent a year on the Blackpool promenade in a barrel with an act in which he had to starve himself as close to death as possible. Davidson ended up in Skegness preaching the Bible from inside a lion's cage. Unfortunately, in 1938, he was mauled by a lion and he died a few days later. Beach performers would build a wooden stage in sight of the pier, and afterwards catch money in nets on long poles from spectators in the 'gallery'.

Skegness was where Billy Butlin created the first purpose-built holiday camp. Opened in April 1936, he quickly increased the number of timber chalets from 500 to 1,200. By the end of that first season he had 2,000 there. During World War II, Butlin's Skegness holiday camp was taken over by the Royal Navy as HMS *Royal George*. My late father Stanley Wood was stationed there in 1943. He recalled that leaving the camp was referred to as 'going ashore'.

In 1940 the pier was deliberately breached against the threat of invasion. It re-opened in 1948 after repairs costing £23,528. The severe floods of 1953 damaged the pier head which had to be rebuilt at a cost of £3,000. In 1971 a new entrance was built, which included a café, shops and an amusement arcade, and the theatre was extended to seat 1,100. It had been said, unkindly, that the original entrance kiosks with their Gothic archways would have been 'more at home in a cemetery!' Two large sections of the pier were washed away by a storm on 11 January 1978, cutting off the sea end and leaving the pier-head theatre and eastern shelters high and dry. When plans to link the two sections with a monorail and build a new 1,200-seat theatre and a 250-foot tower fell through in 1985, it was decided to demolish the pier head and the theatre. While this was being done, for safety reasons, the building was gutted by fire.

The shore end of Skegness Pier has continued to flourish and, in 1991, a tenpin bowling alley was added with other facilities including a children's soft play area and 'Laser Quest!' In 1997 staff at the bowling alley claimed to have seen a ghost. They christened it 'Salty'. The winter of 2005/6 saw the completion of a phased re-decking and refurbishment of the pier head at a cost of about a quarter of a million pounds.

Frantic fun at one end, peaceful pursuits at the other (author's collection)

Skegness Pier, c.1904 (Frances Foote collection)

CHRIS'S VERDICT: frantic fun at the shore end, calm and peaceful thereafter
WALK TIME: 1 min 13 sec

Work started: 1880
First opened: 4 June 1881
Designer: Charles Clarke and Robert Pickwell (their only pier)
Contractor: Head Wrightson
Construction: screw piles, cast iron columns, iron lattice girders and bracings
Original length: 1817 ft (554 m)
Present length: 387 ft (118 m)
Landing stage: yes
Storm damage: 1882, 1953, 1978
Ship collisions: 1919
Fire: 1985
Restoration: 1898, 1929/30, 1936/9, 2005/06
Legal: Skegness Pier Orders 1879 & 1946
Original owners: Skegness Pier Co.
Present owners: UK Piers Ltd.
Website: www.skegnesspier.co.uk

SOUTHEND-ON-SEA

Southend Pier on fire, Thursday, 29 July 1976 (courtesy of the Southend Pier Museum)

WORLD'S LONGEST PLEASURE PIER

Southend Pier in Essex suffered a major fire in October 2005, but recovered to be voted Pier of the Year in 2007. Give yourself plenty of time to visit Southend Pier, at least two hours, or half a day if possible. As with any pier, the more leisurely visitor can take all day. Not only is Southend the world's longest pier, it has a great deal more to offer. Of course, technically it is not a seaside pier, being on the north bank of the River Thames, but the river is so wide at this point that it may as well be. And, there is the advantage of being able to view both banks of the river!

At one-and-a-third-miles long, Southend Pier is a good hike, even one way. Best idea is to take the electric railway out and walk back, or vice versa according to taste. There are two trains, the *Sir John Betjemin*, named after the Poet Laureate and pier enthusiast, and the *Sir William Heygate* after the Mayor and Alderman responsible for the first Southend Pier in 1829. You are welcomed to the pier by a striking, circular entrance building that is entirely modern in concept and design but looks exactly right for its place and purpose. The shore-end railway terminus is situated at ground level, and the pedestrian entrance at first floor level – but there is bridge access from the town and excellent lifts operate precisely where you need them.

The train journey is remarkably comfortable. The track is single apart from a mid-pier passing place. As the seaward terminus was destroyed in the 2005 fire, a temporary station was put in place. On alighting, you can see just how fierce the fire had been. Massive wooden timbers on either side of the pier have been deeply charred. This was the old end of the pier before it was extended in 1898. The fire destroyed the rail station, the pub, gift shop, amusement arcade, toilets and part of the restaurant. There was £5 million-worth of damage, thankfully covered by insurance! I was assured that all would be restored for the 2008 season, but found the temporary facilities – including toilets – to be excellent.

Southend Pier, c.1920 (Tim Mickleburgh collection)

Walking onto the extensive pier head with its elevated sun deck – another modern construction that looks entirely in keeping with its much older base – you forget just how far you are from land, one-and–a-third miles in fact! Underneath the sun deck is the RNLI shop, well stocked with souvenirs, models, toys, books and jigsaws. Two inflatable rescue boats are on display. The lifeboat station itself is at the shore end of the pier, on the downstream side. It was the busiest RNLI station in 2006 with 146 people rescued, and the fourth busiest in the UK. The 'talking telescope' (50p/£1) tells you what to look for. There are some wartime Mulberry Harbours, the Isle of Sheppey and Canvey Island and much else in between, as well as river traffic.

I was impressed by the number of people of all ages who were walking the length of the pier, and by the number of anglers. Some of these chaps fling their lines over the rail with such brio you fear they might throw themselves into the Thames as well. But closer examination reveals their low centre of gravity. The decking has been fixed by countersunk bolts, making it smooth underfoot. The well-designed litter bins have heavy lids – a real necessity on an open pier deck. For walkers, there are four shelters with seats every quarter of a mile, so you can always break your journey and take a rest. The lamp-posts along the pier are also in harmony. The illuminations set above the rail track perhaps spoil the overall effect, but the view at night is more than adequate compensation.

As a major seaside resort, Southend offers all the usual entertainments in abundance. Right by the pier is Adventure Island, described as 'the UK's No. 1 free admission fun park'. As well as being the word's longest pier Southend claims to have the widest 'shore end' of any pier.

Southend Pier, c.1945. (Frances Foote collection)

Southend's first pier, opened in June 1830, was a modest 600-foot (183 metres) wooden affair. Before that, carts and rowing boats took passengers out to the waiting steamers. In 1846 it was extended to 6,600 feet (2,013 metres), becoming the longest pier in Europe. It had a baggage line, later adapted for passengers. Princess Mary and the Duke of Teck were on the pier on 9 October 1872. In 1875 the Southend Local Board bought this pier for the princely sum of £10,000. The wooden structure had suffered depredation by worms, and the wooden deck had been worn out by horses' hooves. With the old wooden pier becoming increasingly dangerous, the decision was made to replace it with an iron one. Work started in August 1888, pedestrians were allowed on in July the following year, and the new pier officially opened on 24 August 1890. The cost was a massive £80,000, including £10,000 for a state-of-the-art electric tramway, installed by Cromptons of Chelmsford, to take passengers and their luggage to and from the steamships at the pier head. There was a main hall seating 2,000 and an outside bandstand with canvas screens.

With an increase in steamer traffic, it was decided to extend the pier rather than dredge the Thames. The new pier head was opened in January 1898, extending the pier to 7,080 feet, making

Train approaching the south signal box (courtesy of the Southend Pier Museum)

it the longest in the world. In 1908 a promenade deck was added. When the upper deck to the pier extension was officially opened on 25 July 1908 it had 600 permanent seats and room for 500 deckchairs. The lower deck had room for 6,000–8,000 people! There was also a bandstand and six shops. King George V was on the pier on 14 July 1921 and again in 1923. By 1925 the pier was attracting more than one and a quarter million visitors a year. Further extensions to the upper deck were completed in 1927.

On Monday, 8 July 1929 the Prince George Extension was officially opened by HRH Prince George, Duke of Kent, bringing the pier up to its present record length of 7,080 feet. (That's one and a third miles, or 2,159 metres.) An additional line of piles were added to the east of the pier, allowing the rail track to be doubled. At that time, Southend Pier was attracting 1.5 million visitors a year.

Now here's a curiosity: although originally opened in 1830, Southend Pier did not celebrate its centenary until 1935. That's because it was not until 1835 that the Admiralty first included the structure on its charts. During World War II the pier was requisitioned by the Navy who renamed it HMS *Leigh*. The pier, or rather HMS *Leigh*, was fortified with pill-boxes, anti-aircraft guns and depth charges. Searchlights were installed. The electric railway was used to ferry troops and land the wounded. The pier became the centre for the control of all shipping in the Thames and the assembly point for wartime convoys for the duration of the war. In all, Southend Pier sent off 3,367 convoys, involving 84,297 vessels, 50,000 servicemen and 80,000 tons of ammunition and supplies.

When Southend Pier re-opened in May 1945, the public flocked to it in unprecedented numbers. In 1949/50 more than seven million people visited Southend Pier. Four point seven million of those paid to go on the electric tram, and one million to walk the pier. Situated close to the town's railway station, Southend Pier was the focal point for millions of holidaymakers and day-trippers from London and elsewhere. But, by 1970, the numbers had dropped to below a million, although recent attendances of 360,000 visitors a year are still impressive.

In 1950 the pier-head Dolphin Restaurant was built from timber and scrap materials left over by the Navy. Other pier buildings included the Sun Deck Theatre, the Solarium Café, and the Hall of Mirrors. As late as the 1960s, a fleet of thirteen ships operated from Southend Pier, however, due to a decline in trade, the pier's entertainments were franchised in the 1970s. The pier walkway was re-built in the years 1974–1979.

In October 1959 the shore-end pavilion was destroyed in a fire that trapped 300 people on the pier. They were taken off by boat. The pavilion was replaced by a tenpin bowling alley. On 8 August 1965 the Dolphin restaurant was gutted by fire. In July 1967 a major fire destroyed the shore-end pavilion, and also the theatre, cafes and coastguard station. On 11 August 1971, a storeroom and the disused restaurant burned down.

Then there was another huge conflagration. On Thursday, 29 July 1976 a fire began near a restaurant on the lower deck at the pier head. Five hundred people were trapped on the pier. They were taken to safety by train and boat, women and children first. Fanned by the strong south-westerly winds, the fire raged out of control. Seven fire-fighting tugs arrived to help the fire crews. It was a four-hour battle, made all the more difficult and dangerous by exploding diving equipment and ammunition from the rifle range. Pilot Ladislav 'Ladi' Marml helped fight the fire from the air. He flew his tiny crop-spraying aircraft, the tanks of which held 400 gallons of water a time, on numerous 'sorties' over the blazing pier. Eleven fire engines and 100 firefighters were involved. The fire destroyed the theatre, café, amusement arcade, coastguard station and the radar training school. Repairs were estimated at £1.4 million. In 1977 a bowling alley fire cost a mere £200,000!

In October 1978 the pier railway, now a single track, had to be closed for safety reasons, and the pier train was withdrawn. The pier's rolling stock was scrapped in 1982. From a peak of five million paying customers in 1949, by 1970 visitor numbers had fallen to below one million.

When Southend Council voted to close the pier at the end of the 1980 season, there was an immediate public outcry. Starting from scratch, a Pier Festival was organised in three weeks flat. Individuals and local groups combined to form an *ad hoc* Festival Committee to organise the event which took place on 1/2 September 1980 and was a great success. Sir John Betjeman, president of the National Piers Society (NPS), and John Hodgkiss, first NPS chairman, gave their support with Sir John – too ill to take an active role – as the titular head of the campaign. Betjeman declared: 'the pier is Southend, Southend is the pier'. Dick Owen, chairman of the Leigh Heritage Society, was the festival committee chairman, Ronald Dowie was vice chairman and his wife, Peggy, now chairman of the Southend Pier Museum Foundation, was secretary. Widespread support and massive publicity had its effect. With the pier due to close on 30 September, the Council agreed to keep it open until a permanent solution could be found; meanwhile, the pier was to be managed on behalf of the Council by the Lecorgne brothers.

In 1983 the overnment's Historic Buildings Committee granted the Council £200,000 towards the cost of repairing the pier, supplemented further by insurance money. A £1.3 million rescue package saw rebuilding work start in November 1984. A new 36-inch gauge railway with new rolling stock was opened by HRH Princess Anne on 2 May 1986. In 1989 the Southend Pier Museum was opened. The museum, located at the pier entrance, is run by a charitable trust and staffed by volunteers. It is open four days a week from May to October.

Pier entrance, c.1890 (courtesy of the Southend Pier Museum)

Southend Pier, c.1960 (Frances Foote collection)

Vanishing point (author's collection)

Situated on the Thames, it is no surprise that Southend Pier has suffered several ship collisions. In all, nine ships or barges have collided with the pier. In 1891 a wood barge sliced right through the pier. Ships hit the pier in the years 1891, 1898, 1908, 1921, 1933 and 1986. It was a coaster in 1891 and a ketch in 1898, the *Violette* in 1921, and the barge *Matilda Upton* in 1933. On 23 November 1908 the *Marlborough* sliced right through the deck between the old and new pier heads. The pier was relatively narrow at this point, as the pier railway did not reach that far down the pier. In June 1986 the MV *Kings Abbey* also cut through the pier between the old and new pier heads. It shattered six cast iron piles, severed the lifeboat slipway and caused irreparable damage to the boathouse. A 70-foot gap was left in the pier. Repairs costing £0.5 million followed in 1989, with a new café and toilets opening on the stem extension.

On Wednesday, 7 June 1995 yet another fire began with an electrical fault in the bowling alley. Four people trapped on the pier head were taken to shore by by boat. The pier re-opened three days later. The fire also damaged the pier deck and the pier railway was forced to close. In 1996 the pier head superstructure was blasted, cleaned and painted. The fire-damaged area at the shore end was re-built in 1998 by French Kier Anglia Ltd. in. In 2000 a new RNLI lifeboat station and gift shop with sundeck above were built at the pier head. The pier illuminations were switched on for the first time on 17 November 2000, and on Good Friday 2001 the Southend Cliff Lift re-opened and the new sun deck was opened. The Pier Hill Lifts not only make access to and from the pier and the promenade easy, they provide superb viewing platforms across the Thames. In 2003 a new £1.9 million entrance was built with full disabled access.

Bowling Pavilion, c.1964 (Frances Foote collection)

But fire struck once again. On Sunday, 9 October 2005 a blaze destroyed the pier-head station. A 130-foot section of the pier was destroyed. Thirty-three fire engines and 75 firefighters were called out, and damage was estimated at a cost of £10 million. The fire re-ignited on Wednesday, 12 October but was quickly put out. Even after this recent fire damage has been put right, Southend Pier will not rest on its laurels. Yet more developments are planned for the future, so watch this space! MV *Waverley* and *Balmoral* called in 2007.

Southend was voted Pier of the year 2007 after being runner-up in 2005, and second place runner-up in 2006. Southend Pier is the longest in the world, and its pier railway is, needless to say, also the longest in the world.

SOUTHEND-ON-SEA

CHRIS'S VERDICT: the world's longest pier; Pier of the Year 2007 – what more can I say?
WALK TIME: 20 min 14 sec

Work started: (i) 1828; (ii) August 1888
First opened: (i) 1829; (ii) 24 August 1890
Designer: (i) Messrs Walker (their only pier); (ii) James Brunlees
Contractor: (ii) Arrol Bros. of Glasgow
Construction: (i) wood; (ii) cast iron screw piles, steel joists, timber walkway. Pier head: greenheart timber piles.
Extension: reinforced concrete piles
Original length: (i) 600 ft (183 m); 6600 ft (2013 m), 1846; (2) 7080 ft (2159 m), 1929
Present length: 7080 ft (2159 m) [1.34 miles]
Ship collisions: 1891, 1898, 1908, 1921, 1933, 1986
Fire: 1959, 1976, 1995, 2005
Restoration: (i) 1846; (ii) 1945–50, 1960, 1974, 1979, 1984–6, 1989, 2000–01, 2006–07
Legal: Southend Local Board Act 1887
Original owners: Southend Local Board
Present owners: Southend-on-Sea Borough Council
Support group: Southend Pier Museum Foundation
Pier of the Year: 2007 (winner), 2005 & 2006 (runner-up)
Website: www.southend.gov.uk

SOUTHPORT

On the Pier, Southport

Southport Pier deck, *c.*1909 *(courtesy of the National Piers Society)*

UK's SECOND LONGEST PIER

To me, the greatest joy that Southport has to offer – and it has got a lot to offer – lies inside the pavilion at the end of the pier: a real, genuine, old-fashioned, working penny arcade! This is claimed to be the biggest collection of mechanical toys and amusements under one roof. They are all there – the laughing sailor, the haunted churchyard, table soccer, games of skill and chance, tell your fortune, and, yes, the 'What the Butler Saw' peepshows provided by the Mutoscope & Reel Company of New York. All are in working order. All you have to do is to change your money into pre-decimal coinage – ten old pennies for £1. Older readers will know that, prior to 1972, there were 240 old pence to the pound – that's inflation for you!

To get to the end of Britain's second longest pier, you can let the tram take the strain, or take the walk over the Marine Lake with its pagoda-like buildings. There is an actual paddle steamer, a miniature version of a Mississippi paddle-boat rather than the side-paddle type that used to call at the pier in the heyday of sea excursions. But the road train along the promenade only looks like a miniature 'Wild West' locomotive – there is a reliable diesel engine underneath. But it is all good fun! The shoreside Funland is open all the year round, and offers tea and coffee at 30 pence – surely the cheapest in the country? And admission to the pier is free.

When Southport Pier was built in 1859/60, it replaced a former wooden structure that had collapsed into the sea. Southport Pier was the first pier built primarily as a pleasure pier. It is the oldest surviving iron pier. And, as the second longest pier, it is just as well that the pier tram is alive and well. A large crowd watched the first pile being driven on 14 August 1859. Although a Pier Committee had been formed as early as 1852, it was seven years later before work began. The designer was the brilliant railway engineer James – later Sir James – Brunlees. The contractors were W &

J Galloway of Manchester. Using Brunlees' 'jetting' technique, all 237 piles were fixed in only six weeks. The pier measured 1,200 yards in length and was five yards wide, with a 120- by 20-foot platform at the sea end and steps leading down to a landing stage. It cost £9,319.

The pier company was formed in 1859 at a meeting in the town hall and began with £8,000 capital. The official opening on 2 August 1860 was marked with a grand gala, a procession, a banquet, an 'illustration', fireworks and a ball. The only sour note came in a letter to the local newspaper, the *Southport Visitor*: 'The turnstiles [on the pier] are extraordinarily inconvenient for elderly ladies especially, the amplitude of dress rendering it impossible to pass through them without much unpleasantness.' But the pier company had an answer. Ladies should buy a monthly ticket that would allow them access through the gate, thus avoiding the turnstiles.

Huge crowds turned out to watch the procession through the town prior to the opening ceremony. Day trippers came by train from Liverpool for one shilling return. The steamer *Storm King* offered passengers an excursion for two shillings and sixpence, or 15 shillings including luncheon with wine. There was wine too at the celebration banquet on land, including champagne, burgundy, port and sherry. The ball continued into the early hours.

Southport Pier was an immediate success. Promenaders were charged sixpence, bath chairs and sedan chairs a shilling, and prams sixpence. It was three pence on the pier train, plus one penny for every 'trunk, portmanteau box or parcel' up to 14 pounds in weight. A return passage to Barrow was three shillings second class, four shillings first class. The short sea trip to Lytham was one shilling return. By 1910 the return fare to Blackpool was 2s. 6d. (two shillings and sixpence), and to Llandudno 3s. 6d. At its peak, Southport pier was the calling point for 20 steamship companies operating almost 50 services to 15 ports and resorts. The last steamer sailed from the pier in 1923.

Waiting and refreshment rooms for boat passengers were added in 1862. The following year the baggage line was upgraded to a passenger-carrying, cable-operated tramway. It opened on 7 May 1863. The track was re-laid in 1893, and the system was electrified in 1905. Prior to 1863, boat passengers (or their porters) had to haul their trunks and cases over 1,000 yards to the pier head! But passengers still had to walk to catch the steamer until 1865 when 'knifeboard' cars were introduced. Passengers sat back-to-back in the open, and the journey from the pier entrance to the pier head took all of three minutes. It was first operated by steam power, then electricity, then after World War II diesel power, and later by batteries. Now it is diesel again.

The pier was widened in 1864, and in 1868 the pier was extended to a massive 4,380 feet (1,336 metres), not far short of a mile long, to reach the deep-water channel. Paddle steamers operated to and from Blackpool, Fleetwood, Lytham and Llandudno. By 1920 more than 100 fishing boats also worked from the pier.

On New Year's Day, 1902 a new shore-side Pier Pavilion was opened to replace the one burned down in 1897. Marie Lloyd, Harry Lauder, Jimmy James, George Robey, Wee Georgie Wood, Rob Wilton, George Formby (both father and son), the young Charlie Chaplin, Gracie Fields and Vera Lynn played there, among many other stars. There were twice-daily concerts, admission 3d., 6d. and 1s. (that's threepence, sixpence and a shilling). Flanagan and Allan premiered their song *Underneath the Arches*, at Southport Pier in 1929. New entrance buildings replaced the old in 1903.

When 'pioneer aviator' Claude Graham-White landed unexpectedly on Southport sands on 1 August 1910, a large crowd gathered. Within the year, the enterprising local council (and how often do you see those three words together?) had built a hangar and was charging landing fees! Between the wars, the diving *professors* were a popular entertainment with their comic and daring diving displays. One such notable was *Professor* Powsey who set his bamboo bicycle on fire before riding it into the sea. Bert Powsey was 73 when he made his last dive after a career that took him all around the world as well as being an attraction at Southport Pier for over 20 years.

Due to fires and storm damage, Southport Pier has been reduced to 3,633 feet (1,108 metres) in length; still a challenging length and longer than when it was first built. The pier's first disaster came in 1865. One of the tramcars left the line, and Mrs Frances Bateman, a widow, was thrown into the railings. She died within 24 hours. Her brother-in-law John Anderton survived with serious injuries. The Bateman family sued the pier company and were awarded £400, with £250 for Mr Anderton. When the cargo ship *Mexico* was wrecked on the Horse Bank, the pier became a convenient platform to observe the tragedy. Three lifeboats were launched, but two were lost. Twelve sailors were saved but 27 lifeboatmen died. Their dependents received £1 each. In 1889 fierce storms swept away some of the pier foundations and wrecked the refreshment room. The pier head and pavilion were destroyed in an 1897 fire, causing damage estimated at £4,000.

The seaward end was again destroyed by fire on 25 July 1933 when the concert pavilion crashed into the sea. Southport Corporation took over the pier and tramway in 1936 and rebuilt the trams. The pier was closed during World War II when it had a searchlight battery installed. The loss of the town's DC electricity supply in 1950 resulted in the Corporation replacing the old 3 feet 6 inch service with a 23½-inch gauge diesel railway. In September 1950, the schooner *Happy Harry* was driven into the pier by gale-force winds and had to be blown up to remove it. The pier was reduced in length by a 1957 fire, but still remained the second longest. Another fire in 1959 destroyed the pier-head buildings, costing £50,000 in damages.

All aboard for the end of the pier (author's collection)

'When the sea is not at Blackpool' – comment on a postcard, 1906 (Tim Mickleburgh collection)

It's all in the name (author's collection)

Southport Pier 'bicycle dive', 1930s
(courtesy of Sefton
Council Libraries)

In 1990 Southport Pier escaped demolition by only one vote on the local Sefton Council. A Charitable Trust was set up in 1993 and a Friends Group the following year. The forecourt was improved and re-opened in 1994. But problems with funding delayed renovation, and the pier was closed in 1996 when attendances were down to 100,000 a year Eventually the money was found, with the help of the Heritage Lottery Fund and a European Objective One grant, as well as provisions from Sefton Council and the Southport Pier Trust. To have the pier restored to something like its former glory cost a massive £7.2 million. A pier tram, funded by the Mersey Waterfront Regional Park, the Council and the Pier Trust, replaced the old pier train.

The £50 'buy a plank' scheme was supported by the late Queen Mother, Ken Dodd and naturalist David Bellamy. All the contributors were able to add their own personal message to the work, for example: 'Planks for the memory', 'because no town should be pier-less' and 'Southport has no peer'.

Old and new themes were utilised. The lighting and shelters along the pier neck maintain the traditional look, while the ultra-modern, lozenge-shaped pavilion at the pier head is a bit of a shock, but does not look out of place. In just two and a half years since re-opening, Southport Pier has had a million visitors. The quality of the renovation helped Southport gain the National Piers Society Pier of the Year award in 2003. More than 300,000 people a year now visit the restored pier and it is Southport's biggest free attraction. On 19 July 2004, the Earl and Countess of Wessex opened the new Marine Way Bridge and Prince Edward took the train down the pier. 22 August 2005 saw a new tram link between the pier and the town centre.

Two other piers were planned for Southport but were never built.

Pier entrance, c.1910 (courtesy of Sefton Council Libraries)

CHRIS'S VERDICT: everything you want from a classic seaside pier, and the penny arcade!
WALK TIME: 10 min 31 sec

Status: Grade II
Work started: 14 August 1859
First opened: 2 August 1860
Designer: James Brunlees
Contractor: Alfred Thorne
Construction: steelwork
Original length: (i) 3600 ft (1098 m); (ii) 4380 ft (1336 m), 1868
Present length: 3633 ft (1108 m)
Storm damage: 1889
Ship collisions: 1950
Fire: 1868, 1897, 1933, 1959
Restoration: 1890, 1901, 1994, 2001
Legal: Southport Pier Order 1868
Original owners: Southport Pier Co.
Present owners: Sefton Council
Support group: Southport Pier Trust
Pier of the Year: 2003
Website: www.virtualsouthport.co.uk

SOUTHSEA CLARENCE

Ancient cannon guards modern seaside fun palace (author's collection)

WIDER THAN IT IS LONG

Clarence Pier is all front and no back – unless you count the funfair which runs along the beach rather than out to sea. But, like its neighbour the South Parade Pier, there is history here. You can see the memorial to Admiral Lord Nelson, who sailed from here prior to his great victory – and his death – at the Battle of Trafalgar on 21 October 1805. This is a busy shipping channel and all kinds of craft are on view, including the Ryde hovercraft ferry which beaches right next to the pier – definitely worth watching!

The original pier was opened on 1 June 1861 by the Prince and Princess of Wales. The Prince, later King Edward VII, came back to open the pavilion in August 1882. Until 1873, the pier had a tramline that ran from Portsmouth railway station and onto the pier, taking passengers and luggage to the Isle of Wight ferry. From 1866 the Landport and Southsea Tramway ran to the pier. In 1873 the pier station was replaced by the Harbour Railway station. A concrete extension to accommodate the increasing boat traffic was built in 1905, and in 1932 a new café, sundeck and concourse hall were built along with shops on the front.

During World War II, the Clarence Pier was virtually destroyed by enemy bombing, with heavy raids on 10 January 1941 and 1 June 1941. This was Hitler's secret plan to demoralise the British – bomb our seaside pleasure piers! It took some years and a quarter of a million pounds to rebuild the pier. The first pile was driven in 1953, and work on the superstructure began in 1959. The new pier was eventually opened on 1 June 1961 – one hundred years to the day after the original pier was opened. As a 'new build' pier, it counts as Britain's second post-war pier.

Clarence Pier claims to have 'the largest amusement complex on the south coast'. Even so, it is a very short pier – but extremely broad in more ways than one.

Southsea beach and Clarence Pier, c.1900 (Tim Mickleburgh collection)

CHRIS'S VERDICT: just for fun
WALK TIME: 25 sec

Work started: 1860
First opened: (i) 1 June 1861; (ii) 1 June 1961
Designer: (i) Mouchel & Partners (deck and landing stage), A E Cogswell & Son, R Lewis Reynish (super-structure).
Construction: (i) iron with concrete extension; (ii) steel frame.
Original length: 132 ft (40 m)
Present length: 132 ft (40 m)
Restoration: 1905, 1953–60
Present owners: Southsea Clarence Esplanade Pier Co. Ltd.
 Website: www.clarencepier.co.uk

Looks good from the side (author's collection)

ROCK ON, TOMMY!

The South Parade Pier has a homely feel about it. The amusements are aimed mainly at children, although kids of all ages (from one to one hundred and one) can all have fun on piers! The children's funfair on the pier deck is certainly good for young children. There are the usual amusements in the arcade, including bowling. The round pier head has seats all round, and there is a fishing platform.

You do not need the talking telescope to tell you that there are fabulous views from the pier towards Selsey Bill and the Isle of Wight. And, it was from this spot that Henry VIII witnessed the sinking of his flagship the *Mary Rose* on 19 July 1545. Part of an English fleet that sailed out of Portsmouth to engage the French, she fired a broadside and was turning to fire her guns on the other side when she keeled over and sank. The *Mary Rose* was raised in 1982 and is now preserved in Portsmouth's No. 3 dock.

Princess Saxe-Weimar opened South Parade Pier in 1879. It was 600 feet long with raked piles, and replaced an earlier wooden pier. The pier was once Portsmouth's biggest user of electric light! It had to be re-built after a serious fire on 19 July 1904 when the sea-end pavilion burned down. The new pavilion was built on a concrete deck and cost £85,000. It encompassed two halls, one a 1,200-seat theatre and the other a café and dance hall. The new pavilion was opened by the Mayor of Portsmouth, Councillor F G Foster JP, on 12 August 1908. There was also a smaller pavilion, including a bar and lounge, at the pier head.

There was another fire in 1966, and yet another in 1974, during the filming of the rock musical *Tommy*, caused further damage. The pier re-opened in 1975 after a £500,000 rebuild. The large pavilion houses now two show bars and amusements. There are tea dances on Wednesday afternoons at 1–4 p.m.

Southsea South Parade aerial view, c.1954 (courtesy of Northern Writers)

Bathers at South Parade Pier, c.1910 (Frances Foote collection)

CHRIS'S VERDICT: a family pier
WALK TIME: 1 min 45 sec

Work started: (i) 1878; (ii) 1907
First opened: (i) 1879 (ii) 1908
Designer: (i) G Rake (his only pier); (ii) G E Smith (his only pier)
Contractor: (ii) Head Wrightson
Construction: (i) timber; (ii) cast iron trestles under a wooden and concrete deck
Original length (i) 1000 ft (305 m); (ii) 600 ft (183 m)
Present length: 600 ft (183 m)
Storm damage: 1964, 1965
Fire: 1966, 1974
Restoration: 1906/08, 1910–12, 1966/7, 1974/5
Legal: Southsea South Parade Pier Order 1878
Present owners: Six Piers Ltd.
Website: www.southparadepier.co.uk

SOUTHWOLD

SOUTHWOLD

Southwold Pier, 2007 (Bournes collection)

OUR NEWEST PIER

If you want to see something different, then Southwold Pier in Suffolk is the place to go. At first glance Southwold appears to offer little more than a gentle stroll and refreshment in a quiet seaside resort devoid of brash amusements. All very welcome, but then you are invited to experience the 'Under the Pier Show'. You may have heard of the End of the Pier Show, but this show is as different as its name implies.

For a start, you are invited to experience the Bathyscape. There are lots of weird and wonderful coin-in-the-slot machines (some looking distinctly ancient, which just adds to the appeal) and all kinds of unusual games. This is 'hands on' experience at its most bizarre. But there is more! 'Some of our machines have escaped and are trying to make a getaway,' you are warned. Sure enough, 'escaping' along the pier are two more weird and wonderful machines to gladden the hearts of all Heath Robinson fans.

First there is the pier water clock, which 'performs' every half hour but may be turned off during high winds or freezing temperatures. Then there is the Quantum Tunnelling Telescope, which modestly claims to show 'absolutely everything you could possibly want to view through a pier telescope'. Visitors are clearly affected by all this craziness – some have even dropped pennies and 'tuppenny pieces' (I saw no silver) onto the flat tops of the round wooden piles just beyond the pier's sea end, presumably for luck, but just out of reach. What brave person I wonder abseils out over the raging sea to collect the loot? Pier owner Stephen Bournes, using money thrown into the bottom of Tim Hunkin's celebrated water clock, set up a fund – the Southwold Pier Youth Scholarship – to help local youngsters go on exchange trips.

Leaving aside all this madness, Southwold Pier is just the thing if you like quiet recreation. Having a tea or coffee and perhaps a cake on the pier deck, sheltered from the wind and with the sun, sea and shore views to sooth you, is a balm for the soul. Even the litter bins on the pier, discreet in gunmetal grey, incorporate a small but perfectly formed fish motif punched through in a simple but charming pattern.

When the MV *Balmoral* berthed at Southwold Pier in June 2002, it was the first ship to do so in nearly half a century. This pier was built by the Coast Development Company, who operated the *Belle* steamer fleet between London Bridge and Great Yarmouth. Authorised by the Southwold Pier Order of 1899, the 810-foot wooden pier with its T-shaped landing stage opened in the summer of 1900. A wooden pavilion with refreshment rooms was later built at the shoreward end.

The Amusement Equipment Company Ltd. took over in July 1906 when the CDC was succeeded by the Coast Development Corporation Ltd. Belle Steamers continued to operate the London to Great Yarmouth service until 1934 when storms destroyed the pier's T-head. Two years later, a new pavilion – still here today – was built at the shore end. In World War II, not only was the pier sectioned, it was hit by a drifting sea mine. In 1948 the pier was restored at a cost of £30,000. Storms breached the pier in October 1955. The seaward end was left isolated and was later washed away. Another gale in February 1959 saw the pier reduced to only 150 feet in length. In 1960 part of the pavilion became a pub.

The Iredale family bought Southwold Pier in 1987. They renovated the pavilion's first-floor theatre and function rooms and later extended the pier to 500 feet. The former cafeteria re-opened as 'Flipper's Diner', and a fitness studio replaced the old Neptune bar. The pier neck behind the bar serves as a unique beer garden. A fund-raising campaign, started in 1999, raised enough money to extend the pier neck to its present length of 623 feet. The new pier was opened on 3 July 2001 by HRH the Duke of Gloucester. The new T-shaped head was completed later.

As another 'new build' pier, Southwold is our third postwar pier and the 'youngest' of our seaside pleasure piers – and that's official! The pier is open at 10 a.m. every day except Christmas Day. As well as being extremely well run and maintained, Southwold Pier is a handsome pier. Built on plain, round columns with an absence of tracery, it looks homely and welcoming – as does Southwold itself.

The pier's explanatory leaflet is first class and tells you everything you need to know, except who actually runs the pier. The 2007 version tells of future plans: 12 contemporary two-bedroom holiday apartments with rooftop terraces and balconies, refurbishment of the promenade café, boardwalk restaurant and arcade. The flats will be built above the pavilion which is being retained for public entertainment, as now. While building flats and apartments on piers is controversial, it can be argued that this is the only way some piers can be kept in being.

Southwold Pier and beach, c.1924 (Frances Foote collection)

SOUTHWOLD

*Rebuilding Southwold Pier,
2000
(Bournes collection)*

*Quantum Tunnelling Telescope
on the pier-head. It's up to you
to find out what it does!
(Bournes collection)*

*Waverley docked at Southwold
Pier, c.1950
(Bournes collection)*

Southwold Pier – proposed entrance incorporating new apartments (Bournes collection)

CHRIS'S VERDICT: full marks for originality
WALK TIME: 2 min 08 sec

Work started: (i) 1899; (ii) 2000
First opened: (i) 1900; (ii) 3 July 2001
Designer: (i) W Jeffrey (his only pier); (ii) Brian Howard, Nick Haward (project manager)
Construction: timber
Original length: 810 ft (247 m)
Present length: 623 ft (190 m)
Storm damage: 1934, 1955, 1979
Restoration: 1948, 1987/8, 1998, 2000/1
Legal: Southwold Pier Orders 1899–1949
Original owners: Coast Development Co.
Present owner: Stephen Bournes
Pier of the Year: 2002
Website: www.southwoldpier.co.uk

SWANAGE

Swanage Pier, c.1907 (Marlinova collection)

CHARMING AND BENDY, BUT BEWARE THE GRIBBLE WORM!

As well as being charming, picturesque, well-maintained, run by volunteers and in a wonderful setting, Swanage Pier is a bendy pier! Just looking at it is guaranteed to lift your heart and bring a smile to you face. And walking, or rather strolling, along it is sheer joy. Everything, seats, lamps, rails, shelter, is in keeping with its Victorian and Edwardian heritage. There are no garish amusements, just a few from yesteryear.

The Old Pier, 750 feet long, was built in 1859 at a cost of £6,000 to ship Purbeck stone from the Langton Matravers quarries. Horses were used to pull carts along a narrow-gauge tramway along the promenade to the end of the pier. In 1874 George Burt started a steamer service between Swanage, Poole and Bournemouth. As the numbers of trippers increased, it became clear a new pier was needed to cater for the day-trippers as well as the Purbeck stone. The new pier, 642 feet long, cost £10,000. The first pile was driven on 30 November 1895, and the pier was officially opened on 29 March 1897.

The first steamer, PS *Lord Elgin*, arrived on 1 May 1896. Ten steamers a day served Swanage in 1905. Return fares to Bournemouth were 1*s*. 6*d*. in 1899, 6*s*. 6*d*. in 1956 and around £5 in 2002. The last of the old steamers left Swanage on 24 August 1966, but the pier is once again being used for boat trips. Until the 1950s, the old pier was used a diving platform for Swanage Swimming Club. Its remains can still be seen to the right of the existing pier.

The new pier was originally built on 170 imported Greenheart timber piles. Attack from the dreaded gribble worm (a marine wood-boring crustacean) had eroded the piles so much so by 1927 that they had to be protected by reinforced concrete. In 1940 the landward end of the pier was blown up as an anti-invasion precaution. It was rebuilt in concrete in 1948, but the gribble

Remains of the Old Pier
(author's collection)

worm had continued its depredations by eating away to wood between the seabed and high water mark. The last steamer, the PS *Embassy*, called on 24 September 1966 and the pier fell into disrepair. Durrant Developments bought the pier in 1986, but when the company went bankrupt, the pier was put in the hands of the receiver.

The Swanage Pier Trust, run and financed entirely by volunteers, took over the pier in 1994. Since then, the Trust has raised and spent over £1 million in renovating and maintaining the pier. Fifty-seven of the pier's 168 Greenhart timber piles have had to be replaced, and the deck renewed in Ekki wood. The concrete piles have been replaced with timber. The Victorian wind shelter was rebuilt to its original design. The railing panels and the

A 'paddler' alongside Swanage Pier, c.1909 (Marlinova collection)

Volunteers keep Swanage Pier in very good nick.
Note the anglers' facilities on the pier head
(author's collection)

Victorian lamp standards have been recast in iron from original 1896 moulds. Pier Trust patron, Lord Raglan, presided at a re-opening ceremony on Sunday, 27 July 1998. There are regular boat trips to Bournemouth, Poole and the Isle of Wight. The maintenance work continues, but the Trust has to raise £130,000 a year to run and maintain the pier.

There is a small charge to 'stroll' along the pier, but it is well worth paying. In 2001, 82,894 'strollers', 15,734 divers and anglers, and 14,749 boat passengers used Swanage Pier. There is a shop, a small museum, a display of Donald McGill's 'naughty' seaside posters and a room with Edwardian gaming machines (including 'What the Butler Saw') with a supply of old pennies to work them. Anglers are well catered for. At the pier head there are half-a-dozen work benches and even a fishing line bin.

SWANAGE

CHRIS'S VERDICT: a true pier
WALK TIME: 3 min 15 sec

Status: Grade II
Work started: (i) 1859; (ii) 30 November 1895
First opened: (i) 1859; (ii) 1 May 1896–29 March 1897
Designer: (i) Richard St George Moore; (ii) James Walton, London
Contractor: (i) John Mowlem
Construction: (i) timber; (ii) timber, reinforced concrete.
Original length: (i) 750 ft (229 m); (ii) 642.5 ft (196 m)
Present length: 642.5 ft (196 m)
Restoration: 1928, 1997/8
Original owners: Swanage Pier & Tramway Co.
Legal: Swanage Pier Act & Orders 1859–1948; Swanage Harbour Revision Order 2001
Present owners: Swanage Pier Trust
Support group: Friends of Swanage Pier
Websites: www.swanagepier.com, www.swanagepierfriends.co.uk

TEIGNMOUTH GRAND

Just in case you didn't know what it was (author's collection)

SEASIDE FUN SPOT

In the early 1900s, 'Peg Leg Pete' used to set himself on fire before diving into the sea from Teignmouth Pier. There were water-polo matches, watched by spectators from small boats as well as from the pier itself, tea dances and magic lantern shows. The pier featured its 'Famous Ladies Bohemian Orchestra' and, in the 1940s, Evelyn Hardy and her Band. In 1961 the Brenner family took over the pier and introduced more modern amusements, which now include 'high tech' video games.

Before the pier was built, a wheeled platform was used to give access to small boats in summer. Work started in 1865 and two years later the 700-foot pier was complete. It cost £8,000 and was built without the usual Act of Parliament. The pier was the dividing line for male and female bathing: the women's bathing machines were to the east of the pier and the men's to the west. In 1871 Teignmouth Pier was bought by Arthur Hyde Dendy who planned to relocate it at Paignton. When this proved too difficult, a new pier was built at Paignton and Teignmouth pier was restored before being re-opened on 24 July 1876. Pavilions were built at both ends of the pier and excursion steamers called daily during the summer. The pier was enlarged in the early 1900s when a new landing stage was added. In 1904 the pier's entrance kiosks fell into the sea for no apparent reason. In January 1908 high tides and strong winds damaged the shore-end pavilion and caused part of the promenade to collapse.

Sixty feet of the pier neck was removed at the start of World War II. After 1945 the gap was closed by a steel bridge, but later this was removed to leave the pier 75 feet shorter. One of the pavilions burned down, and in the 1960s the pier was in danger of collapse. In 1973 new steel piling was inserted under the buildings, going down 80 feet into the bedrock, and the shore end was repaired. A new groin scheme to protect the beach from erosion had an adverse effect on the pier, undermining the shoreward end wooden piles and exposing their bases. Truckloads of sand and cement had to be brought in to again save the pier from collapse.

Once entitled the 'Grand Pier' which featured on a classic British Rail poster, Teignmouth pier is now announced by the single word 'PIER' in huge letters atop the shore-end pavilion. Inside you will find the usual amusements, but you must pass through the arcade to get to the rest of the pier. Hopefully the side passageways will be re-opened.

The railings and lamp standards are decorated with a sea-horse motif, but one of Teignmouth Pier's best features is the series of excellent information boards at intervals along the deck, adding much to the visit. There are seats and tables at the front of the pier with the admonition 'please do not feed the seagulls'. Quite right too – rats with wings! A further plus for Teignmouth itself is the pristine state of the nearby toilets – sparkling clean and well deserving of their numerous 'Loo Awards'.

Teignmouth beach, c.1955 (Frances Foote collection)

CHRIS'S VERDICT: something for everyone
WALK TIME: 1 min 51 sec

Work started: 1865
First opened: 1867
Designer: Joseph William Wilson
Construction: cast iron screw piles
Original length: 700 ft (214 m)
Present length: 625 ft (191 m)
Legal: Non-statutory
Original owners: Teignmouth Pier Co.
Present owners: Grand Pier Teignmouth Ltd.
Website: www.torguay.com/New_Torquay/local/piers

TORQUAY PRINCESS

A very pleasant promenade pier. Note the courting couple on the left. 'T'was ever thus, with piers!' (author's collection)

OVER THE HARBOUR WALL

Torquay Princess Pier, to give it its full name and title, is actually perched atop the harbour wall with one set of legs in the sea. There are two advantages to this arrangement. One, you can gaze out over the marina and its fancy yachts as you stroll along; and secondly, you can continue your walk right round to the harbour entrance. Strolling – and sitting – are just about the only things you can do on Torquay Pier, but the adjacent town centre has just about everything you would wish to sample otherwise. Then there is the Princess Theatre, a fine modern building set back from the pier entrance. Frankie Vaughan and Joe Pasquale, among many others, have performed here.

There is a gift shop, and you can take the Brixham ferry from the pier end. There is a string of lights down the centre of the pier and seats on both sides. The wooden pier deck has been repaired in places but more work on this is needed.

The harbour groin was built in 1890 and the steel lattice and timber structure on top was added in 1894. The pier-head landing quay dates from 1906. Half the pier head was replaced between 1957 and 1964. The 'Islander' pier-head entertainment building burned down in April 1974 and was demolished. This revealed that much of the steel structure had corroded. Reconstruction work started in 1978 and was completed the following year.

Supreme thriller writer Agatha Christie (my grandmother's favourite author) loved to roller-skate at Torquay. I thought I would share that with you.

Torquay harbour, c.1935 (Frances Foote collection)

TORQUAY PRINCESS

An exciting and challenging building with the promise of stimulating performances within
(author's collection)

CHRIS'S VERDICT: fine for a stroll
WALK TIME: 2 min 19 sec

Work started: 1890
First opened: 1894.
Designer: Alfred Thorne (his only pier)
Construction: steel lattice and timber on mass concrete groin
Original length: 780 ft (238 m)
Present length: 780 ft (238 m)
Restoration: 1906, 1957–64, 1978/9
Present owners: Torbay Borough Council
Website: www.torbay.gov.uk/index/system/panorama-princess-pier.htm

TOTLAND BAY

The pier-head 'pavilion' (a sort of well-appointed shed) is now an artist's studio (author's collection)

HIDDEN GEM

Down a narrow track, and tucked under a cliff you will find Totland Bay Pier, one of four that still survive on the Isle of Wight. The shore-end café is thriving, and you can sit out on the pier and enjoy your meal in the open air. But beyond that, the deck is closed to the public. The decking itself looks in reasonable condition, but the original railings, which incorporated seats running both sides the length of the pier neck, need complete renewal. Owner, Derek Barran, who bought the pier in 1999, is seeking finance to renovate this lovely little pier, but in such a position, commercial opportunities are few and far between. As a private concern the pier is not eligible for lottery funding.

Barran is an artist who uses the main building on the pier head as his studio. The pier is 450 feet long and 14 feet wide. The pier head is 88 feet by 52 feet. The main pier-head building has a separate bunkroom–kitchen with water and electricity. There are steps down to a small landing stage and the pier has its own mooring. On the east side of the pier is a storage room and a small pier-master's hut.

Totland Bay Pier was built by S H & S W Yockney and opened in March 1880, replacing an old wooden jetty which was in a 'ruinous condition'. Its main purpose was to provide access to the Totland Bay Hotel. There was a shelter at the pier head and a small amusement pavilion at the landward end. Ferryboats did call at the pier. In 1916 it cost 1*d.* to disembark at the pier, and the fare from Yarmouth was 6*d.* The ferry service ended in 1927, but pleasure cruises continued until 1931. Like many others, the pier was sectioned in World War II but re-opened on 17 June 1951 when the *Lorna Doone* called. A new pier-head shelter was built in the 1950s.

In the early 1970s, Totland Bay Pier was sold to Trinity House for £10,000. The National Physical Laboratory installed a data-gathering centre in 1975. The amusement arcade suffered fire damage in August 1978 and the pier was closed. Storm damage in October 1987 increased the repair costs to an estimated £1 million-plus. The pier was sold again in 1992, for just £1,000. The MV *Balmoral* called in May 1993, but still repair work was hindered, this time by vandalism. The pier was subsequently sold for £19,500 but remained closed apart from the shore end.

The pier itself is delicately strung along pairs of cast iron piles with cross-bracing supporting the wooden deck. The pier-head piles are made from greenheart and stand proud of the pier by 2 feet, with an additional safety rail all round. The main building on the pier head was restored in 1999 and the small landing stage also restored in 2000. The humble, ranch-style landside building is basic but welcoming. There is limited parking close to the pier, but there is more along the waterfront where – surprise, surprise – you will find the Waterfront Restaurant and Bar. Public toilets are nearby, and there is a nice sandy beach and a few rocks for the young and the young-minded.

The pier looks out onto Freshwater Bay. It is close to the Needles and is a good vantage point for watching yacht races around the Isle of Wight. Totland Bay is a lovely unspoilt bay and attracts many yachts during the summer.

Sadly, the deck is closed to the public (author's collection)

Totland Bay Pier from the beach, c.1930 (Frances Foote collection)

CHRIS'S VERDICT: hidden gem
WALK TIME: n/a

Work started: March 1879
First opened: March 1980
Designer: S H & S W Yockney (their only pier)
Construction: pairs of cast iron piles with cross bracing, steelwork supporting timber deck
Original length: 450 ft (137 m)
Present length: 450 ft (137 m)
Restoration: 1949/50
Legal: Totland Bay Pier Order 1879
Present owners: The Totland Pier, Steam & Navigation Co. Ltd.
Website: www.thetotland_pier.com

WALTON-ON-THE-NAZE

Just about the biggest and brashest pier front I have seen (author's collection)

THIRD LONGEST PIER IN THE UK

Now lets get this straight. The Naze is not a river: it is a headland. *Naze* is the Saxon for nose – it is as simple as that. Walton Pier has two main parts, both huge. At the shore end is an enormous amusement arcade, open all the year round. Painted in eyeball-hurting daffodil yellow, it must be visible from outer space. Behind this massive emporium of fun is one of the longest piers in the UK. You can walk along it, or take the land train.

Just before the end of the pier is an offshoot that houses the Walton & Frinton lifeboat, the Tyne class lifeboat *Sir Galahad* is protected by recently-installed wave screens. Then there is the 'bend at the end' and a large area of boardwalk serving no particular purpose. Here there is sea fishing for cod, whiting, skate, bass, eels, sole, stingrays and dogfish for £5 a day. Seems good value to me. The public address system gets right to the end of the pier – strangely comforting. But why are there so many pigeons?

With the pier neck and sea end strictly for walking, viewing, fishing and the lifeboat station, and no seats other than a few cobbled together from scrap steel and timber by the fishermen for the fishermen, you must take your amusement at the shore end. That is where you will find the bar and plenty of tables for your drinks and eats.

The first Walton Pier, built in 1829/30, was a 300-foot wooden jetty and was used only for landing goods and passengers. In low water, passengers often had to transfer to small boats to get ashore, so it was later extended to 800 feet. Remarkably, it lasted 50 years before being destroyed in a storm in January 1880. A second pier was built at Walton in 1871, but did not last nearly as long. Lack of water at the pier head meant that passengers had to be taken out to the steamers in small boats.

A new iron pier, 2,600 feet long, was opened in 1898. It was owned by the Walton Pier & Hotel Company, another example of Victorian entrepreneurship by combining two facilities. It was built by local engineer Peter Bruff who also worked on the Clifton Hotel and the railway station. The pier had a single-track electric railway 3 feet 6-inch gauge This lasted until 1935 when it was replaced by a battery-powered car. After World War II diesel power was used on a 24-inch gauge line which opened in 1948. The railway was taken up in the 1970s, and now there is a land train.

The pier and the battery car were damaged by fire on 30 May 1942, but the pier was repaired after the war. There were two severe storms in 1978, one at the beginning of the year, 11 January, and the other at the close of the year on 31 December, the latter resulted in a 108-foot gap in the pier neck, cutting off the lifeboat station. This was repaired, but for the most part the New Walton Pier is plain and simple – just very long.

Walton Pier c.1906
(Frances Foote collection)

Walton's state-of-the-art Tyne Class lifeboat moored by
the 2005 wave screen at the end of the pier
(author's collection)

CHRIS'S VERDICT: a long pier with lots of shore-end amusements
WALK TIME: 7 min 49 sec

Work started: (ii) 1895
First opened: (i) 1830; (ii) 1871; (iii) August 1898
Designer: (i) John Penrice (his only pier); (iii) Peter Bruff
Contractor: (ii) J Cochrane
Original length: (i) 800 ft (244 m); (ii) 530 ft (162 m); (iii) 2600 ft (793 m)
Present length: 2600 ft (793 m)
Storm damage: 1978
Fire: 1942
Restoration: 1979
Legal: Walton-on-the-Naze Pier Orders 1864–9, 1897, 1900
Original owners: Walton Pier & Hotel Co.
Present owners: New Walton Pier Co.
Website: www.walton-on-the-naze.com

WESTON-SUPER-MARE BIRNBECK

Birnbeck Pier, c.1900 (Frances Foote collection)

ONLY PIER TO AN ISLAND

This pier has so much history attached to it and it is so unusual, it is a tragedy to see it in such a state of decay. New owners Urban Splash have plans to refurbish the whole structure and bring visitors flocking once more to Birnbeck Island, but even to the layman it is obvious that this job will cost millions. The Friends of the Pier and the Pier Trust have made strenuous efforts over the years to keep it alive, but without an agreed plan and the cash to back it, this wonderful structure can only deteriorate further, out of sight, round the headland.

There are so many stories about Birnbeck Pier. One tale goes like this: 'Notice how the wind seems to be in your face as you go out over the pier, but drops when you get to the island. That is the ghosts of two young boys who were drowned in 1819 after crossing at low tide, long before the pier was even thought of. They're telling you not to go!' Then there is the guy with the loud voice, a very loud voice. He was the 'gull-cryer' who lived on the island when it was used by the fishermen to spread their nets after a fishing trip. He would scare the birds away so loudly, he could be heard as far as Congresbury – ten miles away!

More recently, the eccentric owner of the pier, John Sylvester Critchley, printed his own currency for visitors to buy their food, drink and entertainment. These were all in note form, from a farthing note to a two-shilling note. He put on Victorian evenings on the island in the 1970s and 1980s, and guests would arrive in period costume.

Because of the state of repair, or rather disrepair, the pier is closed to the public. The deck is in a terrible state, but a narrow walkway has been constructed to allow access to the lifeboat station by the island. Because of the huge rise and fall of the tide, this has the longest lifeboat slipway in the country.

But you can view the pier from the Cliffside gardens above, from the adjacent Royal Pier Hotel, and you can get right up to the pier gates where the 'Friends of the Old Pier' have taken over and refurbished a signal-box type structure which was the switching station for the trams that used to run right to the pier entrance. Here you can learn about the pier and buy memorabilia. The remains of a turnstile can still be seen at the pier entrance. You can see the bell tower on the pier master's cottage. The bell was rung every time a ship was approaching.

Birnbeck Pier was built after two previous plans failed to came to fruition. One was for a suspension bridge to the island, with a jetty for steamer landings on the far side. Then there was a madcap scheme to build a huge breakwater. The scheme that did come to fruition was a Birch-designed pier, 1,040 feet long and 20 feet wide, and cost £70,000. The foundation stone was laid on 28 October 1864. The prefabricated parts were made at Messrs Toogood's Isca iron foundry in Newport, Gwent. The ornate, gothic-style tollhouse and pier master's cottage were designed by the notable local architect, Hans Price. The pier opened on 5 June 1867 with a twopence toll for visitors. It was lit in the evenings by gas lamps; the gas was supplied through a pipe that ran across the back of the seats. On the island there were large refreshment and waiting rooms, a water-chute, switchback railway, and swings. But the pier company paid no dividends for the first 17 years. From April 1885 Birnbeck Pier had its own set of by-laws.

A new landing stage was added in 1872, and a lifeboat station in 1881. A tramway was installed to carry baggage to and from the steamers; the luggage line being a tiny car on four wheels on a platform – sit with your knees under your chin and your luggage behind to be man-handled along the pier rail track! A pavilion was built on the island in 1884, only to burn down on Boxing Day, 1897. A new pavilion, designed also by Price, who was also active at Clevedon, was erected the following year, along with a westward jetty.

The Victorians built the huge concrete platform that still dominates the Birnbeck

Advanced decay on pier's right arm
(author's collection)

Pier deck – safe passage for lifeboat crew on right
(author's collection)

Island pavilion getting to the point of no return
(author's collection)

'The Old Pier', c.1912 (courtesy of the National Piers Society)

island. On it was built a series of fine buildings, most of which now seem to be beyond repair, but it was thriving in its heyday. In 1890 local shopkeepers complained that there were 'too many amusements' on Birnbeck Pier. These included an Alpine Railway, a shooting gallery, a photo-studio, tea and coffee rooms, a merry-go-round, swings, a maze, and bandstand, a zig-zag slide, a bar and a 'theatre of wonders'. The amusements of the Edwardian era included a switch-back railway, a helter-skelter, a water-chute with rowing boats on rails, and a flying machine. There was even a bioscope, an early version of moving pictures. Other amusements featured are 'Bedroom Secrets', 'Artists and Models' and 'Parisian Can-Can'.

A new lifeboat station was built in 1902. The landing jetties were damaged in a storm in 1903, and the following year the North Jetty was replaced by a steel one 300 feet long. The Westward Jetty lasted only until 1920. Competition from the funfair on the town's Grand Pier caused the Birnbeck Island amusements to close in 1933. During World War

Birnbeck Pier water chute (courtesy of the National Piers Society)

II the pier came under the Admiralty and was know as HMS *Birnbeck*. Used for trial experiments by the Royal Navy Department of Miscellaneous Weapons Development. The pier was damaged when a Lancaster bomber dropped a large block of reinforced concrete on it.

Regular passenger steamers stopped calling in 1971, the year before Critchley took over. The last pleasure boat to sail from Birnbeck Pier was the MV *Balmoral* on 19 October 1979. Fire destroyed the White Pavilion in 1988, and the pier suffered extensive storm damage in 1990. This exceptionally fine Victoria pier was closed to the public in 1994, and sadly continues to deteriorate as it awaits rescue.

Surely we can't let this unique pier go? (author's collection)

CHRIS'S VERDICT: dying to be rescued
WALK TIME: 2 min 56 sec (by special permission)

Status: Grade II*
Work started: 28 October 1864
First opened: 5 June 1867
Designer: Eugenius Birch
Contractor: Isca Iron Co.
Construction: cast iron columns, steel cross-bracing and lattice work, wooden deck
Original length: 1200 ft (366 m)
Present length: 1040 ft (317 m)
Fire: 1897
Restoration: 1898, 1904
Legal: Weston-super-Mare Birnbeck Pier Order 1896
Original owners: Weston-super-Mare Pier Co.
Present owners: Urban Splash (South West)
Support group: Friends of the Old Pier
Websites: www.birnbeck.co.uk, www.weston-super-mare.com

WESTON-SUPER-MARE GRAND

Grand Pier entrance, 2007 (Robert Tinker collection)

LAST OF THE GREAT PLEASURE PIERS

This pier certainly has a grand entrance (re-built in 1970), and the rest is pretty impressive also. There are shops on both sides as you walk up the broad ramp to the pier neck, which has a central glazed screen with seats on both sides. There is a land train along this quite lengthy pier, but these cars are of 'knife-blade' design and you need to hold on. The pier-head pavilion – a mini Crystal Palace – houses a huge amusement arcade with an upper floor. There are children's amusements at the far end of the pier, and three 'talking' telescopes. There is plenty of scenery around, including the islands of Steep Holm and Flat Holm.

Originally planned in 1880, construction of Weston's second pier finally got under way in 1903. The Weston-Super-Mare Grand Pier Act was passed in 1893, but had to be amended in 1897 and 1899. Local MP, R E Dickinson, drove first pile on 7 November 1903. Six hundred piles and a total of 4,000 tons of iron and steel were needed. The Grand Pier was opened on 11 June 1904. It cost £120,000, and included an elaborate 2,000-seat pavilion with a music hall that staged opera, , Shakespeare, ballet and boxing. There was also an outside bandstand with canvas screens to protect the audience. Originally intended to be a massive 6,600 feet long, the pier was actually only 1,080 feet when built. A 1,500-foot low-water extension was added in 1906, but few boats docked there due to the hazardous sea conditions. Only three ships ever successfully docked there, and the chairman of the steamship company, who was also pier company chairman, withdrew the service. All but 120 feet of the extension was demolished in 1916–18.

Amusements were added in 1926. The pavilion burned down on 13 January 1930. In 1932/3 it was replaced by a new art deco pavilion which housed a funfair instead of a theatre. This is reputed to be the largest pavilion ever built on a pier.

Grand Pier opening, 11 June 1904 (Frances Foote collection)

During World War II, two piers were built on the islands of Steep Holm and Flat Holm in the Bristol Channel. The islands were part of 'Fixed Defences Severn'. Gun batteries and observation posts were built, and linked to the piers by temporary railways. The pre-fabricated piers, both 120 yards long, were erected by the Royal Engineers and the Pioneer Corps. Built to combat 'the Hun', after the war they were – ironically enough – dismantled by German prisoners of war. Five piers can be seen from Steep Holm Island: Burnham, Weston-super-Mare Birnbeck, Weston-super-Mare Grand, Clevedon and Penarth

The entrance was re-built in 1970. In 1993 a £250,000 bowling alley, plus a two-storey Fun House and a Ferris wheel. £350,000 was spent on renewing the deck. The Brenner family have owned the pier since 1946.

Grand pier head theatre, c.1910 (Robert Tinker collection)

WESTON-SUPER-MARE GRAND

CHRIS'S VERDICT: plenty of fun and a fine pier too
WALK TIME: 4 min 05 sec

Status: Grade II
Work started: 7 November 1903
First opened: 11 June 1904
Designer: P Munroe
Contractor: Mayoh & Haley
Construction: cast iron columns, steel cross-bracing, wooden deck
Original length (i) 1080 ft (329 m); (ii) 2580 (787 m), 1906
Present length: 1200 ft (366 m)
Fire: 1930
Restoration: 1932/3, 1970, 1992/3
Legal: Weston-super-Mare Grand Pier Acts 1893–1932
Present owners: Grand Pier Ltd.
Pier of the Year: 2001
Websites: www.grandpier.co.uk, www.weston-super-mare.com

Start of a very pleasant walk around to the pier itself (author's collection)

TALE OF TWO PIERS

As its name implies, there are two parts to Weymouth Pier. The south-side harbour pier – a solid groin – is reserved for commercial use, with ferries to the Channel Islands and France. On the north side is a piled pier built as a promenade pier in the early 1930s. Set back from both is the huge and rather forbidding – positively Stalinesque – Pavilion Theatre, which is to be renovated and (thankfully) given a facelift. Stuck on the front of this overbearing concrete mass is a peculiar front porch, completely at odds with the rest of the building. If ever a building had a carbuncle, this is it. Hopefully, that will be the first to go. The pavilion does have a sundeck with fine views, however, the sun is hidden behind the building in the latter part of the day.

The entrance to the pleasure pier is a long way removed from the pier itself, but it is a very pleasant walk along the shore, looking across to the broad sweep of Weymouth beach. King George III, who holidayed at Weymouth for 14 successive summers, described Weymouth Bay thus: 'I never enjoyed a sight so pleasing'. There are some seats to view the scene, and when you get to the pleasure pier itself, an old toilet block also provides a vantage point.

The pier deck is largely taken up with a two-storey, 1960s-style building, ugly and careworn and very much in need of a fresh coat of paint, but obviously awaiting decisions on its future. For the present, there is an ice-cream bar at ground level and a café on the first floor where you can choose your views to your heart's content. On the other side of the pier is the Old Harbour and the Nothe Fort, still complete with some menacing-looking guns. The pier itself is part stone groin, part concrete piles.

Weymouth has had a harbour pier since at least 1812, but it was 1840 when a new one was constructed of concrete and Portland stone. It was largely rebuilt in timber in 1860 and extended to

Weymouth Commercial Pier, c.1912 (Frances Foote collection)

900 feet. In 1877 a cargo stage was added to facilitate the handling of Jersey new potatoes. In 1889 the Great Western railway (GWR) took over the Weymouth & Channel Islands Steam Packet Co. and added a landing stage and baggage-handling hall. The theatre was built in 1908.

In 1932/3 a new pier was built in reinforced concrete, 1,300 feet long. The promenade pier included shelters, an elaborate diving stage and changing rooms, and was illuminated at night. The

The Old Pile Pier, Weymouth, c.1900 (Richard Clammer collection)

new pier was officially opened by the Prince of Wales, shortly to start his brief reign as King Edward VIII, on 13 July 1933. The original pavilion theatre was destroyed in a fire in 1954, but it was 1961 before the present theatre was completed.

Cross-channel car ferries have used the *Commercial* terminal since 1973. On my visit, two three-masted barques, the *Kaskelot* and the *Earl of Pembroke*, were tied up on the quayside and open to the public for viewing.

While the future of the commercial pier and the pavilion are assured, the same cannot be said for the pleasure pier. The existing structure is to be incorporated and extended as one arm of a vast new proposed yachting marina. This is a bold and ambitious plan by the local council. Ideally, public facilities will be built at the end of the new extension. Most of all, it is essential that the public will still be able to able to walk along the pier, surely the cheapest and most eco-friendly activity ever devised by man. Yacht owners and their cash are very welcome (and their boats are a canny sight too) but it would be wrong if the new pier was to be reserved for their private use.

The whole scheme, which could cost as much as £100 million, was due to start in 2008 to be completed in time for the London Olympics in 2012. There's optimism for you!

First-floor pier-head café: no finer place to enjoy your refreshment (author's collection)

King George III came on holiday to Weymouth every year for 14 years – he loved the place!
Exact replica of his horse-drawn bathing machine to be seen on the promenade (author's collection)

Monstrous pavilion soon to have a face-lift, thank goodness! (author's collection)

It won't be like this for long (author's collection)

CHRIS'S VERDICT: still a pleasure – let's keep it that way!
WALK TIME: 53 sec (pleasure pier only)

Work started: (i) 1840, (ii) 1932
First opened: (i) 1840; (ii) 13 July 1933
Construction: (i) concrete and stone; (ii) reinforced concrete & steel piles
Original length: (i) 900 ft (275 m); (ii) 1300 ft (397 m)
Present length: 1300 ft (397 m)
Fire: 1954, 1993
Legal: Weymouth & Melcombe Regis Corporation Act 1887
Present owners: Weymouth & Portland Borough Council
Website: www.weymouth.gov.uk

WEYMOUTH PIER BANDSTAND

'The New Pier' – Weymouth Bandstand, 1939 (Marlinova collection)

CUT OFF IN ITS PRIME

Weymouth Pier Bandstand claims to be the shortest pier in Great Britain, but this is disputed by Burnham-on-Sea and Cleethorpes. Built in 1939, the rather grand Bandstand has now gone and only the front pavilion remains. This building is firmly entrenched on the land, with just one row of piers, occasionally lapped by the waves, underpinning its outer edge. The question is not whether Weymouth Pier Bandstand is the shortest pier in the country, but whether, like Burnham, it should be classed as a pier at all.

Yet this was a classy if not classic construction. A competition run by the Royal Institute of British Architects attracted 26 entries. It was won by V J Venning, who designed a pier just 200 feet long, supporting a semi-circular bandstand. Building Weymouth Pier Bandstand utilised 3,000 tons of concrete, 180 tons of steel, 5.5 miles of electrical conduit, 2,500 feet of neon tubing and 1,200 light bulbs. It was opened on 25 May 1939. The band concerts were very popular, but when the rains came only 800 of the 2,400 seats were under cover.

In the 1970s, facilities included amusements, a restaurant and giftshop. However, the bandstand became too expensive to maintain, and both it and the seaward end of the pier were demolished in May 1986. Two schoolgirls won a national competition to 'press the button' and set off the explosion. That left the front pavilion, which has some art deco features, in splendid isolation. The sign on the beach warning 'beware underwater obstruction' suggests the remains of the Bandstand still lurk beneath the surface.

Today, there is a café with tables on the pier forecourt, a restaurant, shop and amusements. There are beach huts nearby, and the beach itself has plenty of sand as well as pebbles. There seems little or no chance of this pier ever being restored to its former, if short and brief, glory. And sometimes the waves do actually reach the Bandstand's one line of piles.

*A touch of art deco on the pier pavilion
(author's collection)*

Weymouth Pier Bandstand, beach and pier, 1960 (Marlinova collection)

CHRIS'S VERDICT: cut off in its prime
WALK TIME: 9 sec

Work started: 1938
First opened: 25 May 1939
Designer: V J Venning (his only pier)
Construction: reinforced concrete and steel piles
Original length: 200 ft (61 m)
Present length: 48 ft (15 m)
Present owners: Weymouth & Portland Borough Council
Website: www.weymouth.gov.uk

WORTHING

Enjoying the sun on Worthing Pier, c.1950 (Frances Foote collection)

CLASSIC PLUS

Worthing Pier's very impressive front entrance and pavilion heralds a classic Victorian pier in harmony with its more modern additions. Smart and simple railings, equally smart lamp standards with single globes, the shelter along the spine and the 1930s-style mid-pier pavilion, all sit happily together. The 'jazz- style' pavilion with its square clock face is a delight. There is nothing garish about Worthing pier.

The pier also has mixture of structures: concrete beams under the shore-end pavilion, triple iron trestles supporting the neck, and square timbers for the lower fishing platform. As well as seats, deckchairs and telescopes. There is an upper-floor viewing platform around the sea-end pavilion, but no shops.

Worthing pier opened on 12 April 1862. Although the pier was popular with promenaders, it was not until 1874 that a nine-piece orchestra was engaged to play three hours a day, weather permitting. In 1881 two shelters were built and a German Band from the Rhine was hired to entertain on a daily basis. In 1888/9 the deck was widened from 15 feet to 30 feet and the head increased to 105 feet. This was to accommodate a landing stage and the 650-seat Southern Pavilion built. The pier re-opened on 1 July 1889. Steamers could only call at high tide, but proposals to extend the pier in 1900 were abandoned. Even if the pier had been doubled in length, the water at the pier head would have been only six inches deeper!

On the evening of Easter Monday, 22 March 1913, the McWhirter Quintet was performing to a small audience of about 30 hardy souls. As the winds rose to 80 mph, the concert was rapidly concluded and audience and players all battled back to shore. Shortly after midnight, most of the pier deck collapsed into the sea. The pier head with its isolated theatre, dubbed 'Easter Island', was marooned. Repairs were made, and the pier was re-opened by the Lord Mayor of London on 29 May 1914. Nine weeks later Britain declared war on Germany.

In 1921 Worthing Corporation bought the pier for £18,978 15s. Visitors were charged 2d. which included admission to hear the orchestra in the Southern Pavilion. A new shore-end 'North' pavilion costing £40,000, was opened in June 1926. The amusement arcade with its art deco clock was built in 1935, and a new 'nautical-style' building, built at a cost of £18,000, was opened on 3 August 1935. It replaced the South pavilion which had been destroyed by fire on 10 September 1933. Hundreds of trippers, many still in their bathing costumes, assisted the fire crews by ripping up the timber decking with crowbars and pickaxes to stop the fire spreading along the pier.

The new pier-head building had a solarium with special glass to enhance the sun's rays, and a first floor balcony. The southern pavilion had hosted concerts of light classical music provided by the only remaining municipal orchestra in Britain. It then became a bar, then a nightclub, and it has also been a cinema as well as once housing a small zoo. In 1937 a central screen was erected along the pier neck, and a Central Pavilion built to house an amusement arcade.

Art deco mid-pier building with its 'Jazz Clock'. It's half past three, nearly time for tea! (author's collection)

A landside pavilion to delight the eye (author's collection)

Worthing Pier, 1937 (Frances Foote collection)

Pier entrance, 1915 (Andy Williams collection)

New amusements, 1983 (Andy Williams collection)

Worthing Pier wrecked, 2 March 1913 (Frances Foote collection)

Steamer services stopped during World War II, which also saw the pier sectioned and two bays blown up. The shore-end pavilion became a forces recreation centre, and the pier was used to embark troops on D-Day in 1944. The pier was partly re-opened in June 1946, but materials for repairs were in short supply. Recycled cast iron water mains were pressed into service as replacement piles. The pier did not fully re-open until April 1949 when steamer services also resumed. In 1959 the Denton Lounge was added to the North Pavilion at a cost of £9,000. In 1963–9 the majority of the timber members on the landing stage were renewed, and in 1979–82 the North Pavilion was refurbished and the sub-structure renewed at a cost of £1 million. More substructure work was needed and the Central Pavilion renovated in 1983/4. Worthing Pier was officially re-opened to the public on 15 February 1985.

The southern pavilion has been unused since 2005, when the nightclub was closed. As a teenager, Bob Monkhouse came second in a talent contest on Worthing Pier. Actor and entertainer, Jon Pertwee, a one-time 'Dr Who', has also performed at the Pier Pavilion Theatre. Currently Worthing Council is replacing the timber decking along the entire length of the pier. This work is due to be completed in 2010. The MV *Balmoral* and the paddle-steamer *Waverley* visit around six times a year.

c. 1852

Early view (Andy Williams collection)

WORTHING

CHRIS'S VERDICT: a happy mix of styles
WALK TIME: 2 min 52 sec

Status: Grade II
Work started: 4 July 1861
First opened: 12 April 1862
Designer: Sir Robert Rawlinson (his only pier)
Construction: concrete, iron and timber
Original length: 960 ft (293 m)
Present length: 984 ft (300 m)
Storm damage: 1913
Fire: 1933
Restoration: 1888/9, 1913/14, 1925/6, 1935, 1946–9, 1963–69, 1980–2, 1983/4, 1985, 1995–present
Original owners: Worthing Pier Co
Legal: Worthing Pier Order 1920
Present owners: Worthing Borough Council
Pier of the Year: 2006
Website: www.worthing.gov.uk

Yarmouth pier head, c.1905 (Ian Dallison collection)

FIGHTING THE GRIBBLE WORM!

Yarmouth pier was built by the town Corporation in 1875/6. An earlier plan by the London & South Western Railway Co. to buy Yarmouth Castle and build the pier from there was squashed by the War Office who refused to sell the castle. The Corporation accepted the lowest of 12 tenders, at £2,250. The pier is set direct to magnetic North, as required by the Crown on granting the site. The Mayor, Dr C W Hollis, opened the pier on 19 July 1876. It was used as a terminus by the Lymington ferry service, and operated by paddle steamers which had been using a slipway on the quay since 1830.

Only three weeks after it had opened, the steamer *Prince Leopold* did extensive damage to the pier as she came alongside on a clear, fine day, smashing through 150 feet of pier deck. The Corporation wrote an extraordinary letter to the shipowners, the Southampton & Isle of Wight Steam Packet Co, apologising for the accident and congratulating the skipper, Captain Beazley, on not doing more damage. In other words (and I translate freely): 'We're very, very sorry that our pier got in the way of your ship. Please accept our apologies. It won't happen again'!

Complaints by local fishermen that the pier gates blocked their traditional access to the beach were ignored by the Corporation, so, one night in July 1877 a group of them destroyed the gates with axes and hammers. The Corporation took the ringleaders to court and won the case, only to find that the canny fishermen had taken the precaution of selling their boats and other property to their brothers and sons. They had no assets to seize, so the Corporation had to pay its own costs. In addition, the judge ruled that in future the gates must not interfere with the right of way to the foreshore.

The opening of the Freshwater, Yarmouth and Newport railway in 1889 brought more visitors to Yarmouth. Before the railway, travelling from Newport to Yarmouth by stagecoach took at least

Solid wooden balustrade, just right for leaning and contemplating (author's collection)

three hours. It was while he was on the Yarmouth Ferry in 1889 that Poet Laureate, Alfred Lord Tennyson, then aged 80, composed his famous poem *Crossing the Bar*. In 1890, it was 4*d*. for a ticket to Lymington, 1*s*. for a third-class ticket to Newport, and 2*s*.- to all Island stations beyond that.

In 1884 the railway was extended to Lymington on the mainland, and from then on there was a regular ferry service between Yarmouth and Lymington. Yarmouth Town Council took over the pier in February 1891. They took the decision to improve access to the pier by demolishing the old buildings facing the pier, thus creating Pier Square in 1895.

On Tuesday, 25 October 1909, the 60-ton barge *Shamrock* crashed broadside into the pier during a gale, destroying 50 feet of deck. Describing the collision as an 'Act of God', the shipowner refused

Yarmouth Pier's modest 'side' entrance (author's collection)

Crowded pier deck, 1953 (Ian Dallison collection)

Yarmouth Pier from the air, 1938 (Ian Dallison collection)

Yarmouth pier entrance, 1905 (Ian Dallison collection)

to pay any compensation. The Royal Navy made use of the pier in World War I. In 1927 new waiting rooms, offices and toilets costing £2,000 were built at the pier entrance, paid for by the Town Trust who in 1916 had spent £250 on replacement piles. The Harbour Commissioners took over the pier in 1931, and the first car ferry service started in May 1938. The South Quay was built in 1964 and a new breakwater in 1972.

Since 1951 the pier has been used by anglers, promenaders and excursion boats. The ferries now call at the adjacent harbour berth. The pier entrance is unprepossessing, its friendly character shown by the voluntary 30 pence toll. The pier piles are of greenheart timber, and the deck of Balai wood. All 553 planks have been sponsored by well-wishers. The solid wooden balustrade is just made for leaning on and contemplating the view, or just contemplating. The 1930s-style lighting columns down one side are just right for this six-foot-wide, strictly pedestrian pier. The small, square pier head, set to the right, has a small shelter for the anglers. The pier was given listed status in 1975.

As a wooden pier, Yarmouth has suffered from attack by the gribble worm which has destroyed 50 piles. In 1980 the Harbour Commissioners considered closing the pier, but withdrew the required parliamentary petition in the face of local opposition. By 1991 a critical condition had been reached. People 'bought' planks at £100 a time, contributing towards the total cost of restoration of £350,000. Another £400,000 was needed; helped by a £250,000 Heritage Lottery grant. After extensive renovation work, the pier was re-opened by author and television presenter Alan Titchmarsh, High Sheriff of the Isle of Wight and patron of The Pier Appeal, on 26 April 2008. This should secure the pier for another 40–50 years.

In the early 1900s, there was an extraordinary proposal by the South Western and Isle of Wight Junction Railway Co. to dig a two and a half mile tunnel under the western Solent to link the Isle of Wight to the mainland at Lymington. The Solent Tunnel Project was approved by Parliament but was eventually abandoned, thus ensuring the future of the Yarmouth ferry service which continues to this day. As well as the regular service to 'North Island', Yarmouth still has visits from the PS *Waverley* and the MV *Balmoral*.

CHRIS'S VERDICT: perfect for promenading
WALK TIME: 1 min 59 sec

Status: Grade II
Work started: May–June 1875
First opened: 19 July 1876
Designer: Denham & Jenvey
Contractor: J Denham
Construction: timber throughout
Original length: 685 ft (209 m)
Present length: 609 ft (186 m)
Ship collisions: 1876, 1909
Restoration: 1927, 1983–86, 1993/4
Legal: Yarmouth Pier Order 1874; Yarmouth, Isle of Wight Pier & Harbour Order 1931
Original owners: Yarmouth Corporation
Present owners: Yarmouth Harbour Commissioners
Website: www.yarmouth-harbour.co.uk

ACKNOWLEDGEMENTS

My grateful thanks go to everyone who has helped me with this book. I am particularly indebted to Tim Mickleburgh for his unstinting support; his hard work in checking information in the text and supplying images from his collection; for his helpful suggestions, and his unfailing good humour. I must also thank my wife, Frances, not only for her support, as always, but also for her enterprise in putting together her extensive postcard collection – an essential element of the book.

CREDITS

Frances Foote; Tim Mickleburgh, Martin Easdown, Richard T Riding, Tim Phillips and Frances White of the National Piers Society; Pearl Mina at Six Piers Ltd.; Bournemouth Borough Council; The De Vere Grand, Brighton; Marks Barfield Architects; Noble Organisation; Peter Orpen; Andrew Dixon; Janet Vaughan; Rob Silverstone; Linda Strong; Poppyland Publishing; Ray Norman; Chris Bond (Cornovia); Gravesham Borough Council; Colin Tooke; Mike Bundock (www.pierheadpublications.com); White Horse Ferries; Wightlink Ltd.; Craig Ollerton (www.olle.co.uk); David Clarke; Martin Easdown (Marlinova Collection); Friends of Queens Pier; St Annes Pier Co.; Sandown Fire Station; Southend Pier Museum Foundation; Sefton Council Libraries; Barry Vaughan.

Aberystwyth Royal: Lee Price; **Bangor Garth:** Victor Glossop; **Beaumaris**: Geoff Lowe; **Blackpool (Central, North & South)**: Ted & Ann Lightbown; **Bognor Regis**: Angie Edlin; **Boscombe & Bournemouth**: Andrew Emery; **Brighton Palace**: Anne Martin, Tony Gibbons; **Brighton West**: Rachel Clark, Fred Gray, Peter Orpen, Sharma Hadrill, Vivienne Newlands, Andrew Dixon; **Burnham-on-Sea**: Louise Parkin, Mark & Catriona Newman; **Clacton**: Mark Baird; **Cleethorpes**: Robbie Marklew; **Clevedon**: Linda Strong; **Colwyn Bay Victoria**: Steve Hunt; **Cromer**: Ian Hall, Keith Deacon, Peter Stibbons; **Deal**: Ray Norman, Nigel Chandler; **Eastbourne**: Ted & Ann Lightbown; **Falmouth**: Chris Bond; **Felixstowe**: Andrew Green; **Fleetwood**: Joey Blower; **Gravesend Town**: Graham Cole; **Great Yarmouth Britannia**: Craig Hilton, Colin Tooke; **Great Yarmouth Wellington**: Malcolm Hewitt, Colin Tooke; **Hastings**: Laurence Bell; **Herne Bay**: Karen Monticelli, Mike Bundock, Harold Gough; **Hythe**: Gail Sharpe, Margaret Swain, Gerry Barton, Lester Lay; **Llandudno**: Ted & Ann Lightbown, Craig Ollerton; **Lowestoft South**: David Clarke; **Mumbles**: John Bollom; **Paignton**: Richard Stevens; **Penarth**: Phil Carradice, Colin Smith, Alan Roy Thorne, Caroline Spiller; **Ramsey Queens**: James Stokoe, Fred Hodgson; **Ryde**: Sean Millward, Elaine Wilkinson; **St Annes**: Amanda Baxendale; **Saltburn**: Tony Lynn, Paul Castle; **Sandown Culver**: Geoff Pidgeon, Colin, Trudy & Clarice Baldock; **Skegness**: Caroline Wilkinson, Amanda Hewitt; **Southend**: Peggy Dowie, Lynn Jones; **Southport**: Harold Brough, Matthew Tinker; **Southsea Clarence**: Jill and Jimmy Norman; **Southsea South Parade**: Ted & Ann Lightbown, Penny Pink, Jez McLees; **Southwold**: Stephen & Antonia Bournes; **Swanage**: Russ Johnson; **Teignmouth Grand**: Anthony Brenner, Viv Wilson; **Torquay Princess**: Derek Singleton; **Totland Bay**: Derek Barran; **Walton-on-the-Naze**: Andrew Green; **Weston-super-Mare Birnbeck**: Mike Davies; **Weston-super-Mare Grand**: Robert Tinker; **Weymouth Commercial/Pleasure**: David Stabler, Richard Clammer, Colin Ellis; **Worthing**: Andy Williams, Kate Loubser; **Yarmouth**: Chris Lisher, Ian Dallison.

ABOUT THE AUTHOR

Chris Foote Wood was born in Prestbury, Cheshire in December 1940, the first of four children of Helen and Stanley Wood from Manchester. The Wood family settled in Bury, Lancashire. Chris's youngest sister, the comedienne, writer and comic actor Victoria Wood, has several times been voted the UK's funniest woman. Their late father Stanley was a successful author and playwright.

Chris was a scholarship boy at Bury Grammar School, 1950–59. He won an open scholarship to Manchester University, but instead took a BSc honours degree course in civil engineering at King's College, Newcastle upon Tyne, then part of Durham University, 1959–62. Chris completed the course but was not awarded a degree.

After various civil engineering jobs, including a spell as bridge engineer on the A1(M) Durham motorway construction, in 1968 Chris set up his own publishing business, Durham Free Press, pioneering local free press newspapers in the UK. He gave up the venture in 1971 and had one further civil engineering job on the A19 Teesside construction for four years, before returning to journalism as a freelance writer and broadcaster. In 1974 Chris set up his own regional press agency, North Press News & Sport, and ran it for thirty years. He sold NPA in 2004 and is now a full-time freelance writer and publisher. Chris is currently "ghost-writing" the autobiography of Glenn McCrory, the only professional boxer from the North East ever to become a world champion.

Chris wrote his first regular newspaper column at the age of sixteen, reporting athletics for the *Bury Times*. He wrote for his college newspaper *Courier* and edited the student arts magazine *Northerner*, making it profitable for the first (and perhaps the only) time. Chris Wood married Frances Foote (now OBE) in 1977, adding her surname to his by deed poll. They have no children, but Chris has three children from his first marriage and two grandchildren.

NATIONAL PIERS SOCIETY

The National Piers Society was founded in 1979 under Sir John Betjeman, at a time when some of our finest piers were threatened with demolition. Over the years the Society has grown steadily and has become well established as the leading authority on piers. Through its efforts, several piers that would otherwise have vanished, remain for the enjoyment of everyone.

The Society's aims are to promote and sustain interest in the preservation and continued enjoyment of seaside piers. It publishes a Guide to British Piers and a quarterly magazine, and advises heritage bodies, lottery boards, local authorities and the media on pier matters. It maintains links with the British Association of Leisure Parks, Piers and Attractions (representing pier owners) and the Paddle Steamer Preservation Society, whose ships operate excursions from pier landing stages. The Society has instituted an award scheme for engineering achievement in pier restoration. It organises visits and talks and holds its Annual General Meeting in a different resort each year. In the longer term, the Society wishes to establish a network of regional branches and a National Piers Museum.

"It is the task of the National Piers Society and its Journal to keep a watchful eye on the condition of our piers, to give advice when asked, and to act as a pressure group to obtain national funds when outstanding piers are in danger"

– John Russell Lloyd, NPS Chairman 1988–91.

The National Piers Society is a registered charity. To join, contact Neville C Taylor, Flat 1, 128 Gloucester Terrace, London W2 6HP. Tel: 0207 262 5898; Email nevtaylor@freeuk.com

Visit the NPS website: www.piers.co.uk

LIST OF PIERS BY COUNTY

ABERYSTWYTH ROYAL – Ceredigion
BANGOR GARTH – Gwynedd
BEAUMARIS – Anglesey
BLACKPOOL CENTRAL – Lancashire
BLACKPOOL NORTH – Lancashire
BLACKPOOL SOUTH – Lancashire
BOGNOR REGIS – West Sussex
BOSCOMBE – Dorset
BOURNEMOUTH – Dorset
BRIGHTON PALACE – East Sussex
BRIGHTON WEST – East Sussex
BURNHAM-ON-SEA – Somerset
CLACTON – Essex
CLEETHORPES - Lincolnshire
CLEVEDON – North Somerset
COLWYN BAY VICTORIA – Clwyd
CROMER – Norfolk
DEAL – Kent
EASTBOURNE – East Sussex
FALMOUTH PRINCE OF WALES –
    Cornwall
FELIXSTOWE – Suffolk
FLEETWOOD VICTORIA – Lancashire
GRAVESEND TOWN – Kent
GREAT YARMOUTH BRITANNIA –
    Norfolk
GREAT YARMOUTH WELLINGTON –
    Norfolk
HASTINGS – Kent
HERNE BAY – Kent
HYTHE – Hampshire
LLANDUDNO – Gwynedd

LOWESTOFT CLAREMONT – Suffolk
LOWESTOFT SOUTH – Suffolk
MUMBLES – West Glamorgan
PAIGNTON – Devon
PENARTH – South Glamorgan
RAMSEY QUEENS – Isle of Man
RYDE – Isle of Wight
ST ANNES – Lancashire
SALTBURN – Cleveland
SANDOWN CULVER – Isle of Wight
SKEGNESS – Lincolnshire
SOUTHEND-ON-SEA – Essex
SOUTHPORT – Lancashire
SOUTHSEA CLARENCE – Hampshire
SOUTHSEA SOUTH PARADE –
    Hampshire
SOUTHWOLD – Suffolk
SWANAGE – Dorset
TEIGNMOUTH GRAND – Devon
TORQUAY PRINCESS – Devon
TOTLAND BAY – Isle of Wight
WALTON-ON-THE-NAZE – Essex
WESTON-SUPER-MARE BIRNBECK –
    North Somerset
WESTON-SUPER-MARE GRAND –
    North Somerset
WEYMOUTH COMMERCIAL/
PLEASURE – Dorset
WEYMOUTH PIER BANDSTAND –
    Dorset
WORTHING – West Sussex
YARMOUTH – Isle of Wight

OTHER BOOKS BY CHRIS FOOTE WOOD

Tindale Towers – New Art Deco Mansion (Northern Writers, 2008)
How Mike Keen's dream home was planned, designed and built 2005–2007. Lavishly illustrated, over 200 colour photographs.

When I'm Sixty-Four – 1001 things to do at 60+ (Capall Bann 2007)
An inspirational lifestyle book for active older people.

Proud to be a Geordie – the Life & Legacy of Jack Fawcett (Dysart Associates 2007).
Authorised biography of a miner's son who became a successful developer. Private publication, not for sale.

Baghdad Trucker (Northern Writers, 2006)
True-life adventures of a long-distance truck driver on the most dangerous roads in the world. As co-author, with Kevin Noble.

Nellie's Book – the early life of Victoria Wood's mother (Sutton Publishing, 2006)
Foreword by Victoria Wood. Growing up in real poverty in industrial Manchester in the 1920s and 1930s.

Land of the 100 Quangos (North Press, 2002)
An exposé of the 100-plus appointed and largely unknown government-funded organisations who run the North East.

Kings of Amateur Soccer (North Press, 1985)
Official centenary history of Bishop Auckland Football Club, ten times FA Amateur Cup winners and the most famous and successful amateur soccer club of all time.

Bishop Auckland in Old Picture Postcards (European Library, 1985)
Local history in words and pictures.

(Further details available at: www.writersinc.biz)

REFERENCES AND FURTHER READING

(arranged alphabetically by title)

A Brief History of Southend Pier, Southend-on-Sea Borough Council 2002.

Adventures in Shrimpville – Pegwell Bay as a seaside resort, Martin Easdown, Marlinova 2005; reprinted Michaels Bookshop Ramsgate 2006. ISBN 190547766X.

A Fateful Finger of Iron – the ill-fated Ramsgate Promenade Pier in a resort history of the town, Martin Easdown, Michaels Bookshop Ramsgate 2006. ISBN 1905477651.

A Guide to Collecting Seaside Pier Postcards, Martin Easdown and Richard Riding, Hythe & Radlett 2006.

A Tale of Three Piers – Blackpool, Jon de Jonge, Lancashire County 1993. ISBN 1871236282.

A Walk Across the Waves, Michael J Burrell, Pear Tree Cottage 1998. ISBN 0953309304.

Beside the Seaside, Bill Pertwee, Collins & Brown 1999. ISBN 1855856948.

Beside the Seaside: a social history of the popular seaside holiday, James Walvin, Allen Lane, London 1978. ISBN 071390744.

Birnbeck Pier Weston-super-Mare, Stan Terrell. North Somerset Museum Service 1996. ISBN 0901104108.

Brighton Between the Wars, James S Gray, B T Batsford Ltd 1976. ISBN 0713431156.

British Piers, Richard Fischer, Thames & Hudson 1987. ISBN 0500 541 256.

Cleethorpes Pier and Promenade, Tim Mickelburgh, North East Lincolnshire Council 2000. ISBN 0953439542.

Cliff Railways of the British Isles, Keith Turner, Oakwood Press 2002. ISBN 0853615942.

Designing the Seaside, Fred Gray, Reaktion Books 2006. ISBN 1861892748.

Fresh Air and Fun: the story of a Blackpool Holiday Camp, Bertha Wood, Palatine Books 2005. ISBN 978187481361.

Fresh air and fun: a Blackpool miscellany, Bob Dobson and Doreen Braithwaite, Landy 1988. ISBN 0950769231.

Guide to British Seaside Piers (third edition), Timothy J Mickleburgh, pub Piers Information Bureau 1998. ISBN 1 871708 03 6.

Herne Bay's Piers, Harold Gough, Pierhead Publications 2002. ISBN 0953897761.

Memories of St Annes Pier on its Centenary 1885–1985, Paul Cantrell, Handbook Publishing 1985. ISBN 0947873007.

Pavilions on the Sea: a history of the seaside pleasure pier, Cyril Bainbridge, Hale 1986. ISBN 0709027907.

Pertwee's Promenades and Pierrots, Bill Pertwee, Westbridge Books 1979. ISBN 0 7153 7794 9.

Pier Railways and Tramways of the British Isles, Keith Turner, Oakwood Press 1999. ISBN 0853615411.

Piers and Other Seaside Architecture, Lynn F Pearson, Shire Publications 2002. ISBN 0747805393.

Piers of Disaster – Seaside Pleasure Piers of the Yorkshire Coast, Martin Easdown, Hutton Press 1996 ISBN 1872167810.

Piers of Kent, Martin Easdown, Tempus Publishing 2007. ISBN 9780752442204.

Piers of the North, Tim Mickleburgh, pub Mickleburgh 1998. ISBN 0951812718.

Piers – Photographic Memories, Tim Mickleburgh, Dial House 1999. ISBN 0711026556.

Piers, the Journal of the National Piers Society, Issue Nos 71–84 (Spring 2004 – Summer 2007).

Seaside Architecture, Kenneth Lindley, pub Hugh Evelyn 1973. ISBN 238789837.

Seaside Piers, Simon H Adamson, pub B T Batsford 1977. ISBN 0713402423.

Southend Pier, Martin Easdown, Tempus Publishing 2007. ISBN 978 0752442150.

Souvenir Guide, Constitution Hill Aberystwyth, Constitution Hill Ltd 2004.

Striding boldly – the story of Clevedon Pier, Nigel Coombes, Clevedon Pier Trust 1995. ISBN 0952521601.

Sun, Sea and Sand, Steven Braggs and Diane Harris, Tempus Publishing 2006. ISBN 075243964 2.

Teignmouth Pier – a pictorial history, Viv Wilson, pub Wilson 2003. ISBN 0953952320.

The End of the Pier Book – a pictorial record of Redcar and Coatham Piers 1871–1979, Peter Sotheran, A A Sotheran Ltd, Redcar, 1981. ISBN 0905032128.

The English at the Seaside, Christopher Marsden, Collins 1947.

The English Spa 1560–1815, a social history, P M Hembry, Athlone Press, London 1980. ISBN 0485113740.

The English Seaside in Victorian and Edwardian Times, John Hannavay. Shire Publications 2003. ISBN 0747805717.

The Great British Pier, Francis Frith Collection, Bounty Books 2007.

The Llandudno and Colwyn Bay Electric Railway, Keith Turner, Oakwood Press 1993. ISBN 0853614504.

The Piers, Tramways and Railways at Ryde, R J Maycock and R Silsbury, Oakwood Press 2005. ISBN 0853616361.

The Romance of the Old Chain Pier at Brighton, Ernest Ryman, Dyke Publications, Brighton 1996. ISBN 0950975680.

The Sail of Cardiff Bay Volume Two, Alan Roy Thorne, St David's Press 2007. ISBN 9781902719191 .

The Story of Cromer Pier, Christopher Pipe, Poppyland Press 1998. ISBN 094614852X.

The Story of Swanage Pier, Olive Middleton 2007.

Threatened Piers, Tim Mickleburgh, Piers Information Bureau 1990. ISBN 187170801X.

Threatened Piers – the saga continues, Tim Mickleburgh, Piers Information Bureau/National Piers Society 1992. ISBN 1871708028.

Times of a Troubled Pier – a brief history of Scarborough's Promenade Pier, Martin Easdown, Marlinova 2005.

Trams beside the Seaside, Keith Turner, Gwasg Carreg Gwalch 2004. ISBN 0863818935.

Walking on Water: the West Pier story, Fred Gray, pub Brighton West Pier Trust 1998. ISBN 0950408255.

What the Butler Saw, Harold Brough, pub Harold Brough 2006 ISBN10 0955478006, ISBN13 9780955478000.

Wonderlands by the Waves, John K Walton, Lancashire County Books 1992. ISBN 1871236193.

Worthing Pier, Dr Sally White, Worthing Museum & Art Gallery 1996. ISBN 0906834112.

A selection of newspapers:

Brighton Argus, Brighton Herald, Isle of Wight County Press, Preston Chronicle, Sussex Daily News, Weston Gazette

Some interesting websites:

www.engineering-timelines.com
www.geograph.org.uk
www.piers.co.uk
www.pier2pier.org
www.theheritagetrail.co.uk